Annie's Attic Mysteries®

Gunns & Roses

Karen Kelly

Annie's®
AnniesFiction.com

Gunns & Roses

Library of Congress-in-Publication Data
Gunns & Roses / by Karen Kelly
p. cm.
I. Title
2012910977

AnniesFiction.com
800-282-6643
Annie's Attic Mysteries®
Series Editors: Ken and Janice Tate
Series Creator: Stenhouse & Associates, Ridgefield, Connecticut

10 11 12 13 14 | Printed in China | 9 8 7 6 5 4 3

— 1 —

"LeeAnn will never believe this without proof!" Annie Dawson positioned her digital camera to capture in pixels the bumper crop of vegetables spread before her—green beans, cucumbers, summer squash, and cherry tomatoes.

A few snapshots later she repositioned herself to include part of her home, Grey Gables, in additional photos. "There. Now she can't protest that this vegetable patch was from someone else's garden."

Annie could hardly blame her daughter for the expected disbelief. Every day since planting the garden, she had anticipated something killing off the plants before harvesttime. This, indeed, had happened each time she had tried growing vegetables while raising her daughter in Texas. LeeAnn had taken to teasing her mother anytime they entered a home-and-garden store with, "Mom, just step away from the veggie seeds!" Who knew that moving to Stony Point, Maine, would make such a difference in her vegetable cultivation ability?

Just wait until you open the homemade pickles I send you, Annie thought, an impish grin lighting her face as she tucked the camera into a pocket of her jeans. Both hands on her hips, she surveyed the bounty, considering how to gather the day's harvest.

A gentle breeze off the harbor at Stony Point teased the soft curls of her blonde-gray hair. Stony Point had become her hometown since the death of her grandmother, Elizabeth "Betsy" Holden, and Annie's inheritance of Grey Gables, her grandparents' Victorian home. The notoriously changeable Maine weather was serving up a fine August day on a sunbeam platter. But it would be wise to pick the vegetables before her adopted state decided to change the menu.

"That's it!" Annie turned on a heel and strode toward the back door of the house. Pausing to stomp any loose dirt from her shoes, she hoped the harvest basket she had just remembered seeing in the attic was as large as she was thinking.

The screen door clicked behind her; a gray cat looked up from lapping water out of a bowl in the kitchen. The word lapping didn't do justice to the dainty procedure, though. To Annie it always looked like Boots, Betsy's cat that Annie had also inherited along with the Holden estate, merely lowered her head near the dish, and water droplets leapt nimbly onto her tongue. Not once had she ever seen water dripping from a whisker or found water on the floor. It wasn't that Boots never caused some occasional mayhem, but water was never an element.

The cat stared at Annie as she crossed the kitchen on her way to the hallway. Annie paused only long enough to stoop down for a quick stroke on the top of Boots's head. Before the cat could rise up on all fours, she had already moved past. "I'm on a mission, Boots! There will be time for play later." Had she not been so focused, Annie might have felt the cat's stare pierce her back like a Lilliputian spear.

Up two flights of stairs, Annie paused as she entered the attic, trying to remember where the harvest basket was perched. A vague impression urged her to the left along the wall, as much as the stacks of miscellany and furniture jumbled there allowed. "Ah, that's right. I moved it when I came up for the garden stakes." She took another step forward, looking for the battered side table on which she had placed it, but Annie halted with a jerk as her peripheral vision caught a glimpse of gray fur.

"No, no, no, Boots and I will not have more mice in our home," she cried. "Grey Gables is not a hostel for roaming rodents." Annie gingerly reached over to a nearby shelf to grab the cracked pottery bowl resting on it. Trying to stalk as much like her cat as possible, Annie flipped the bowl over to capture her prey as she came closer. She bent lower, preparing to spring forward before the mouse could run. Squinting, she placed the bowl on the floor near her feet.

"What on earth?" Annie said aloud.

As she bent closer, it became more obvious that whatever was on the floor was not living. And it was not a mouse. Pushing an old three-legged stool aside, Annie could see more of the wayward creature, which was actually ... a purse. The strangest purse she'd ever seen.

Annie picked it up, surprised at the sleek softness of the fur. Its shape almost formed a circle. At the top, an interlacing pattern decorated a sterling silver clasp in serious need of polishing. Three tassels adorned the front. Opening the clasp, she peered inside and then reached in to pull out a number of silver bands. Annie held one of the bands up to the light. Corroded like the clasp, she could still tell the piece was etched with an intricate design. After setting the band on the stool, she examined the rest of the bands and found them to be three different sizes, but all were etched. Even with the bright summer light streaming in the eyebrow windows Annie could not discern what the lines of etching formed.

Sitting back on her heels, she counted eight silver pieces cradled in the palm of her hand. Annie cast a bemused look heavenward. "You've done it again, Gram!" she said. "Another mystery left in the attic for me." As a child spending summers at Charles and Betsy Holden's Maine home while her parents traveled on missionary work overseas, Annie had spent many an afternoon playing in the attic. It became her private magical land, filled with curiosities. Now that she was a grandmother herself, the attic continued to bring excitement of almost magical proportions into her life.

The mysteries from the attic over the past few years had provided much-needed diversion since the loss of her husband, Wayne, to a massive heart attack. Annie carefully slipped the silver bands back into the purse and stood, thinking of how unmoored she had felt after selling the car dealership she and Wayne had built into a thriving business in Texas and for which she had been the bookkeeper. With both her husband and her work gone—and with LeeAnn now married and a mother—Annie had almost drowned in the void.

The inheritance of Grey Gables upon Gram's death had been the lifeboat back to the land of the living for Annie. Her days filled again with purposeful activity—renovating the old house, renewing her relationship with her childhood friend, Alice MacFarlane, who lived in the carriage house next door to Grey Gables, and immersing herself in the community of Stony Point. The transition had brought its fair share of obstacles and frustrations, but it had also brought joy. And apparently, it had also endowed Annie with a new green thumb for vegetable gardening.

Smiling, Annie found the side table where the harvest basket was perched and carried it and the purse downstairs. Placing the purse on a side table in the living room, she took the basket into the kitchen for cleaning. While wiping the basket with a spray of homemade wood cleaner, Annie hummed to distract herself from the thought of the purse's awaiting mystery. Being a gardener required discipline and disciplined she would be. So she hummed *Come, Ye Thankful People, Come* and redirected her thoughts to the bean and cucumber plants awaiting harvest; that would free up more growing room. She would have plenty of time afterward to polish up those silver bands and see what design lay beneath the tarnish.

With the basket hanging from the crook of her arm, Annie returned to the sunny patch. She had just placed the basket on the ground and bent over the first bean plant when the hedges bordering the side of her yard rustled. Alice emerged through a small gap between two bushes.

Annie straightened and waved at her friend. "Alice, come see my summer miracle!"

The morning sunlight caught Alice's auburn hair, burnishing it with gold as she strode across the grass. She stopped at the edge of the garden, examining it from one end to the other and then exaggerating a frown. "What, no beanstalk soaring higher than the clouds?"

"I said miracle, not fairy tale." Annie grinned and flourished her hand over the plants. "Can you possibly *not* be amazed at the fact that I've managed to not kill off my vegetables? Look at all these green beans and cukes!"

Alice's blue eyes opened wide. "Oh, *that* miracle. How could I have missed it?" She couldn't hold back a chuckle.

"Well, it's before noon. Your brain doesn't generally fire on all cylinders so early," Annie teased back.

"Guilty as charged, though the coffee should be kicking in any time now." Alice bent over to get a closer look at the beans dangling from a plant. "These will be good in a tasty pasta salad! Need some help picking?"

Annie nodded. "Absolutely. There's a pile of cucumbers that needs harvesting too. I still can't believe how well everything is growing, and I know I have you to thank for it. If you hadn't mentioned where Gram kept her gardening notes hidden in the library, I'd probably be mourning yet another vegetable garden gone bad." She gently stabilized a plant between two fingers and pinched a long slender bean off with her thumb and forefinger.

"It would have been shameful to let all the gardening wisdom Betsy gained over the years disappear from your family," Alice said, selecting a bean plant and starting to pick. "She was always making adjustments each growing season to find out what worked best. Honestly, your grandmother was a one-woman house-and-garden network. I'm so thankful she told me about the notes. Who knows how long it would have taken for you to just stumble across them, tucked in the back of that drawer."

Annie started to tell her friend about the purse she had found in the attic earlier, but she then thought better of it. One whiff of a mystery and her garden help would desert her in an instant to look at the find. Instead, she told Alice about the photos she planned to email to LeeAnn and the pickles she planned to make.

"Did you find Betsy's pickle recipes in her recipe box?" asked Alice. She closed her eyes. "Mmm, my mouth is watering just thinking of them! Labor Day just wasn't official without Betsy's pickles at the picnic." Like Annie, Alice still missed Betsy Holden terribly. After her marriage to the charming but chronically unfaithful John MacFarlane had crumbled to pieces, and she had moved into the carriage house next to Grey Gables, Annie's grandmother had been a steady source of love and wisdom for the younger woman.

Annie eyed the plant she was harvesting for any

wayward bugs like the copper-colored Asiatic Garden Beetle or for any holes gnawed into the leaves. "Yes, I found it. If I don't manage to kill the pickling cucumbers or mess up the recipe, I'll be sure to put a jar or two aside for Labor Day. Of course, I have to send some down to LeeAnn and her family." Annie smiled, thinking of LeeAnn and her husband Herb Sorensen and their darling twin children, John and Joanna. Pleased to see that the plant showed no signs of insect invasion, she reminded Alice to be on the lookout as well.

"If today is any indication, you'll have enough cucumbers for an army of pickle jars," Alice declared, peering over at the abundant cucumber plants as she dropped a handful of the beans into the harvest basket. "Maybe even enough to pay your field help in pickles."

Annie moved to the next plant and settled into a rhythm of support, pinch, support, pinch. "If my field hand continues to show up to help, I'm sure it can be arranged. I don't want to keep you from your own work, though." A self-employed consultant for Divine Décor, a home-decor company, and Princessa, a jewelry company, for many years, Alice worked hard in her business, and Annie kept herself mindful of not intruding on her friend's work hours.

"That's not likely to be an issue," Alice assured Annie. "August is usually my semi-vacation month anyway—the calm before autumn and the Christmas rush. Besides, who doesn't want to spend more hours outdoors in this weather?"

Annie released another handful of beans on top of the mound already crowding one side of the basket. "This Texas transplant has fallen in love with August in Maine. In Texas, August is even more brutal than July. A cool front might plunge the temperature all the way down to 91 degrees. It's not a month for comfortable outdoor activity." She squatted down by the last of the bean plants. "Do you have any plans for fun during your semi-vacation?"

"Not yet," Alice answered as she peered at the undersides of leaves to check for signs of insects. "Want to tag along if I come up with anything interesting?"

One last bean separated from its stem and rested in Annie's hand. "Sure, as long as it doesn't involve leaving town for more than a day or two. The garden is beginning to produce too well to neglect it now." Emptying her hands once more, she turned toward the cucumbers. "Now, it's on to the cucumbers."

"You know, if the cucumbers pickle well, you can branch out to pickling other things—crab apples, peaches, beets, peppers," Alice suggested, as she picked from the insect-free bean plant. "I'm particularly fond of pickled peaches, just in case you're wondering."

Annie raised an eyebrow. "Do you see any peach trees here? Or crab apple?"

"There are a couple of farms not too far from here that have pick-your-own days in August." A dreamy look came over Alice's face. "So delicious!"

"You might want to wait and see if my pickling skills are up to par before turning me loose on peaches."

Annie moved the harvest basket closer to the cucumber plants and started at the end of a row, looking for cucumbers that were dark green and firm, with the spiny points smoothed out somewhat but not yet flat. Mushy pickles would definitely not do justice to Gram's recipe.

Alice carried her last handful of beans over to the basket. "Well, your success at duplicating Betsy's rose hip jelly recipe gives me hope for the pickling." She turned her attention to the second row of cucumber vines. Spotting a perfect candidate, she freed it from the vine. The two friends picked in silence for a while, thoroughly content in their chore as the pleasant breeze softened the warm sunshine.

Alice looked down at the small mound of cucumbers beside her, and making a pouch with her oversized T-shirt, filled it with the vegetables to carry to the basket. "This was one of Betsy's baskets, wasn't it? It looks familiar, though it's been a few years since I've seen it."

Glancing at the basket and the bounty her friend had helped her pick, Annie answered, "Yes, I brought it down from the attic earlier, knowing it would be useful if the garden continues to thrive." She paused. "It wasn't the only thing I brought down." Annie paused again, a mischievous light dancing into her eyes.

Her friend's second pause caught Alice's attention from the cucumber vines, and she looked up. "Really? And what else did you bring down from the infamous attic?"

"The most unusual purse I've ever seen with some

thingamajigs inside," answered Annie. "But, go ahead, see for yourself. It's on a side table in the living room."

Her grin widened as Alice sprang up as though attacked by a swarm of fire ants and dashed for the house.

2

Annie combed over the remaining vines to find the last of the cucumbers. Stacking two more atop the respectable pile filling the side opposite the beans, Annie hefted the basket and carried it toward the back steps, stopping long enough to knock the garden dirt from her shoes on the iron boot wipe before climbing the steps. Once inside the kitchen, she transferred the beans into a large colander for rinsing.

Alice charged through the doorway from the hall, her excitement palpable as she flourished the purse. "Annie, this is no purse!" she exclaimed. "It's a sporran!"

Annie dropped a handful of beans into the colander. "It's a what-an?" she asked, as she wiped her hands on a towel and turned around to face her friend.

"A sporran, an outside pocket for a kilt. You do know what a kilt is, don't you?" Alice teased.

"Oh course I do, but apparently I'm less familiar with kilt accessories. Do you know what those things are inside the … sporran?"

Alice opened the sporran's clasp, removing the silver bands. "That I don't know. They aren't part of a kilt, though." Lifting the palm of her hand closer to her eyes, she examined the pieces. "I can't make out the design of the engraving."

"Neither could I," said Annie, taking one of the bands

from Alice's palm. "They're in serious need of polishing. Let me finish washing the vegetables, and then we can polish the bands." Giving the band back to Alice, she turned on the cold water and drew the spray nozzle out to rinse the beans. "Do you know what kind of fur the sporran is made of? When I first saw it, I thought I was glimpsing a gray mouse or rat, but it's not anything like mouse fur up close."

Alice set the silver bands on the kitchen table and then stroked the smooth silver-gray fur. "I'm ninety-nine percent certain it's made of sealskin. The majority of sporrans used to be made of sealskin; it's very durable and waterproof."

"'Used to'?" Annie turned off the water and gently shook the colander to help the water drain more quickly.

Alice nodded slowly. "Ayuh. Government regulations blocked the importation of sealskin into the United States. Now, when was that?" She ran a thumb over the sealskin, as though it was a memory stone. "Sometime in the 1970s, maybe. John's family was talking about it over a holiday meal one year. And by talking, I mean arguing."

Annie took a handful of cloths from a drawer and spread them out on the counter. She moved the pile of beans over to dry and placed the cucumbers in the colander to give them a thorough wash. Raising her voice over the sound of the spray, she said, "What is it about large family meals that brings out the worst in some families?"

"Well, you know John's never been what one would call self-controlled." Alice stared down at the sporran, fingering the three tassels. "We all have a lack of self-control in one area or another, I guess."

"One of mine would be your baked goods," said Annie.

"I guess it could be far worse than having to make sure a few extra pounds don't creep onto my hips." For a moment she felt regret for not having kept in touch with Alice during those two decades when she had been married to Wayne and raising their daughter. How she wished she could have been a support to her friend when she was suffering as her marriage to John deteriorated. Annie knew wishing changed nothing, but she was determined to never let anything come between her and Alice again, as long as she had anything to say about it.

"And how," Alice said, nodding. "Anyway, the sporran has to be at least thirty or forty years old. I wonder when your grandparents got it. Have you seen any kilts around the old place?"

Annie lined the freshly cleaned cucumbers in rows on the towels. "No, I haven't, and I don't remember ever seeing one when I was spending summers here, either, but that doesn't mean there's not one to be found. You up for helping me look in the attic?"

"Sure." Alice glanced down at the tarnished bands on the table. "Which do you want to do first, clean the silver or hunt for the kilt?"

After a moment of consideration Annie answered, "Clean the silver. I really want to see what the engravings look like." She washed the colander and placed it in the drain board, and then turned around to lean against the counter. "The tarnish is heavy and I'm concerned about damaging the pieces. Any suggestions?"

"I haven't been with Princessa for as long as I have without picking up some tricks of the trade." Alice picked up one of the bands to examine the metal again. "This is sterling silver, not silver plate. So I'd suggest using the electrolytic method."

"Impressive. Have you actually done this before?" Annie asked.

"Believe it or not, I have. More than once, in fact. If we are as precise with the method as you are with your crochet, the tarnish should clean up nicely without causing any harm to the pieces. Even better, I'm almost certain you already have everything we need."

Annie knew Alice wasn't one to claim expertise when she didn't actually have it. "Wonderful!" she exclaimed. "Let's get started. What do we need?"

"A large pot, aluminum foil, that colander over there, a plastic spoon, a towel, water, baking soda, salt, liquid dish soap, and measuring cups. Oh, and your stove." Alice ran through the process in her mind once again, making sure she hadn't forgotten anything. "That's everything."

Annie pointed over to a lower cabinet. "Grab the stockpot." She reached up into her baking cabinet and pulled down the baking soda and salt. Once all the needed items were gathered on the counter by the sink, she said, "OK, what's next?"

Alice explained, "First, we need to line the pot with aluminum foil. And I mean completely cover the sides and bottom with the shiny side facing out." She handed Annie the roll of foil. "While you do that, I'll measure out the baking soda, salt, and soap." After all the hours Alice had spent at her friend's house she knew the Grey Gables's kitchen almost as well as Annie did. She plucked the needed measuring cups from the neat stack in the drawer next to the stove. The mound of baking soda had just reached the top of the quarter cup when her head popped up.

"Hey, I remember someone having a kilt!"

"You're not going to make a joke about Tartan, are you?" Annie finished smoothing the foil around the bottom of the pot and began lining the sides.

Alice barked out a laugh. "No, I'm not talking about our mayor's dear schnauzer. I mean you."

"Me?" Annie's eyes narrowed for a moment as she delved back into her growing up years, and then they widened again. "I can't believe you remembered that before I did."

Alice turned the bottle of dish soap upside down over a cup and squeezed. "How could I forget such a fashion statement? Black Watch pattern, I think it was."

"More likely the J.C. Penney pattern," Annie said, pressing the edges of the foil strip down over the lip of the pot. "How I loved that skirt! Though I never told anyone, when I outgrew it, and my mother donated it to the missions clothing drive, I cried. I wanted to make some pillows out of it."

Alice snapped the lid of the soap closed and replaced it by the sink. "I always wondered how hard it must have been for you, being separated from your parents so often when they went on missionary trips. Having some things all your very own would have been really important."

Annie nodded. "It was important that they were portable things too—I needed things I could tuck into my suitcase when I went to Aunt Susan's in Texas or here. My desire to make those pillows was definitely sparked by wanting to keep something special with me when I couldn't keep my parents. I knew they had a good reason for being away, but it didn't make it easier." Running her hands around the inside of the pot, she made sure there were no gaps in the foil. "Here you go, one aluminum-plated pot." She carried it over to the stove.

Alice examined her friend's handiwork. "Good. Now we make a most delectable soup." One by one she poured in the water, soap, baking soda, and salt. Selecting a plastic spoon from the large crock on the counter, she stirred the concoction to mix the ingredients thoroughly. "Hand me the bands, Annie."

Annie gathered the bands and gave them to Alice. She placed them in the pot and moved the pot over one of the burners on the stove, turning it on low. "Now, we wait until it boils for a few moments, and then we'll switch off the heat and let it sit for about five minutes."

Annie picked up the sporran off the table and ran a finger over the silver clasp. "How are we going to clean this? We can't submerge this in your soup, even if seals are marine animals."

"Do you have an old toothbrush with soft bristles?" asked Alice, keeping an eye on the pot for signs of boiling. "We'll also need toothpaste or more baking soda and some soft towels."

"Does any brand of toothpaste work? I always keep my old brushes; they come in handy for so many things."

When Alice assured her that any brand of toothpaste would do, Annie ran upstairs to grab the two items. Alice looked up from the pot when she stepped again through the kitchen door. "This is going to boil any minute. We're only five minutes or so away from seeing what the design is."

"Great!" Annie set the toothpaste tube and toothbrush on the table and rifled through her supply of towels for the softest ones she could find. "I assume I'll be covering the clasp in the toothpaste and using the toothbrush to work it into the details?"

"You got it." Alice eyed the contents of the pot; small bubbles were beginning to rise. "Do you have any painter's tape tucked away somewhere? You might want to cover the bulk of the sporran in plastic wrap and then secure it with the tape as close to the silver as you can get it." While she was speaking, she allowed the mixture to boil for a few moments and then reached over to switch off the heat and turned the oven timer to five minutes.

Annie was spreading a couple of the cloths over the table for a work area. "Good idea." She stopped to poke her head and one arm into the darkness just inside the basement door, re-emerging with a roll of wide blue tape. "Painter's tape is another one of those multi-use items, so I like to keep it handy." As she passed the bakers rack, she plucked a roll of plastic wrap off a shelf on her way back to the table.

"Let me give you a hand while the soup is working its magic." Alice left her position by the pot and held the plastic wrap in place while Annie taped it down, carefully slipping the edge of the tape under the rim of the silver on both sides of the sporran.

The body of the sporran protected, Annie twisted the top off the toothpaste tube and squeezed a pearl of the white paste onto one side of the clasp. She wrapped a cloth around two fingers and began spreading the paste over the metal.

The whiney buzz of the timer sounded. Alice jumped where she stood looking over Annie's shoulder and darted over to switch it off. Placing the colander in the sink, she drained the mixture, leaving the bands in the bottom of the strainer. "This is where I have to be really meticulous," she said, using the spray nozzle to douse the bands as she picked them up one by one. "If you leave any salt behind, it will eat through the silver over time."

Annie looked up from the sporran. "Did it work? Is the tarnish gone?"

Alice spoke over the sound of the spray. "Worked better than a charm. Cool design. I'll show you as soon as I get them all completely goop-free." She squinted at a band she had picked up, checking it over for any signs of residue, and set it on the cloth spread out beside the sink.

The kitchen took on a quiet air of industry as Annie worked the paste into the grooves of the sporran clasp, and Alice thoroughly rinsed and dried all the bands. After disposing of the aluminum from the pot, Alice gathered up the bands and sat down next to Annie at the table.

"Mmmm, you smell so minty fresh." Alice grinned as she held a band in front of her friend's face so she could get a good look at it. She slowly turned the band to show all the parts of the design.

A soft gasp escaped Annie. "Wow, that's some craftsmanship!"

"Isn't it? I've never seen a design exactly like this, but it's definitely Celtic. See the knotwork that resembles the edging of the sporran clasp?"

"The bird is amazing," Annie murmured. "Looks like a

bird of prey, but which one? A rose is clasped in its talons. Are all the bands the same?"

"Yes, the exact same design. I don't think it's an eagle judging by the shape of the head, but I need help to narrow it down more." Alice leaned closer to look at the sporran. "The paste seems to be working well. I can see the clasp design is also definitely Celtic—see the Celtic cross?—other than the knotwork, I don't see any other common elements between it and the bands."

Annie picked up the toothbrush to work the paste into the last section of the clasp. "While I finish cleaning this, why don't you grab the laptop from the library and see if you can find out anything about the band design."

Alice snapped a finger and replaced the band she had been holding among the others on the table. "Excellent idea," she said. "Be right back." She disappeared through the kitchen door, returning a moment later with the laptop. Soon she was tapping away on the keyboard, typing key words into a search engine.

"There—the whole thing is pasted," Annie announced. "How long should I leave the paste on the silver?"

Alice glanced over the top of the computer. "You can probably start removing it from the first side you covered. Try the edge to test it and use warm water to make sure you completely remove the paste."

Annie set the pasty cloth aside and went to the sink to fill a glass bowl with warm water. Setting the bowl on the table, she sat, dipped a new cloth in the water and went to work on the first corner of the clasp. "It worked! The tarnish is wiping right off. Finding anything?"

Alice chuckled. "Yes, I've discovered Celtic designs are quite popular for tattoos." She clicked through a link. "Oh, here's something. Common Celtic bird designs are the crow—also known as the death eagle—herons to show fidelity, and peacocks for symbols of immortality and purity."

"Interesting, but no matches with our design." Annie rinsed out her cloth and dipped it into the bowl again. "The clasp has some kind of plant sprig for the main design. It's repeated on either end of the Celtic cross in the middle with the knotwork connecting them. There aren't any birds."

Alice gave a triumphant grunt. "Ah! Here are some bird-of-prey designs. Eagles are close, but the angle of the head *is* different, like I thought. Here's a kestrel; that looks pretty close. Oh! This one looks similar as well. The design description says it's a hawk." She angled the computer so Annie could see.

The website page contained several pictures of bird designs. Annie leaned closer and pointed at the top one. "Are those two birds biting each other or themselves? I can't quite tell."

"They're biting their own necks, according to the fine print." Alice hovered an index finger between two pictures further down the page. "These are the two I was talking about."

"Sorry, I got distracted by that fascinating, but rather disturbing, design." Annie moved her eyes down the page and bobbed her head. "You're right; they both have a lot in common with the band design. So, it looks like we've got either a Celtic hawk or kestrel ..." she held up the sporran, "and a sprig of ... something. Any ideas?"

Alice peered at the newly polished silver. "Hmmm. My guess is ... I have no idea. My knowledge of plants and trees isn't huge. It mostly revolves around what fits in a window box."

"And we don't even know what the bands *are*. Who do you think might be able to help us?" Annie asked.

Alice slowly closed the laptop, thinking. "Maybe we should start with Mike Malone. After all those years he's spent writing *The Point*, he's a fount of miscellany."

"I'll pop into the hardware store tomorrow and see what Mike can tell me." Annie lifted the sporran closer to her eyes, examining both sides thoroughly. "Now that we have the sporran and bands gleaming, let's head to the attic."

Alice cradled the computer in her arms to return it to the library on the way upstairs. "Right behind you. Hopefully, the attic will provide us with another piece of the puzzle."

3

Annie had always been one to awaken by the sun, rather than by an alarm, which made for some early rising in August. That would be rated disgustingly early by Alice's standards and on the late side for those who manned the many Stony Point lobster and fishing boats, which had already left the harbor for the Gulf of Maine. To Annie, her body timed it just right and gave her the joy of watching the world stretch its arms and shake off the night. It also gave her plenty of time to care for her vegetable garden and her roses. It was a glorious morning, so Annie decided to walk into town to see Mike Malone as soon as he opened his hardware store.

At the top of the rise on Maple Street, the crossroads at Main Street just ahead, she paused long enough to turn and take in the lupines as they festooned the sides of the road with riotous color. No wonder Gram had incorporated the wildflowers into many of her cross-stitch designs; they were as heart-lifting as she had been. Shifting her project bag, which contained the sporran and its contents, to her other shoulder, Annie turned again toward downtown and resumed her walk.

Within minutes she rounded the corner and stepped onto the sidewalk, passing Magruder's Grocery as Mike Magruder was flipping his door sign from "Closed" to "Open." Annie always thought of this section of Main Street as the M&M Way with one Mike owning the grocery store and another Mike the hardware store next to it. Mike number one lifted a hand to greet her through the plate glass window of his store before turning his attention to other chores.

Annie heard the door to Malone's Hardware being unlocked, and a girl in her late-teens opened it, broom in hand.

"Good morning, Kailyn," Annie greeted her. "Is your father in this morning, or are you and Trace manning the store?"

"Hi, Mrs. Dawson," Kailyn answered, her voice cheerful. "Dad's here. Good thing, too, because Trace is M.I.A. Probably stayed up too late playing *Skyrim*."

Annie tilted her head to the right. "*Skyrim*?"

"It's a video game. Gaming is just about the only thing that will keep Trace in one place for more than two minutes. Otherwise, he's outdoors." Kailyn brandished the broom. "And he's missing the one store chore that would take him outside."

Annie patted Kailyn's shoulder, taking care not to snag her ring in the girl's straight, cinnamon-sugar–color hair. "I'm sure your father appreciates your help. And enjoy the sweeping; this morning is as perfect as they come."

"Thanks, Mrs. Dawson." Kailyn opened the door for Annie.

As Annie's eyes adjusted from being in the bright summer sunshine, she heard a door in the back of the store close and a voice call, "You're my first customer of the day, Annie. How can I help you? Boots hasn't shredded any more screens, has she?" As Mike came closer she could see his brown hair—not as thick as it used to be—and friendly eyes.

Annie's green eyes danced. "No. Boots has moved on to more interesting acts of minor destruction." She pulled the project bag from her shoulder. "My most important reason for coming today is to see if you can help me identify something I found in the attic."

"Another Grey Gables mystery?" Mike's eyebrows rose. His hand reached up to tug on his left ear.

"I'm not sure yet," admitted Annie.

Mike waved her over to the front counter. "Well, let's have a look."

Mike made sure his front counter was kept tidy and clean, which was no easy task when running a hardware store in a state full of committed do-it-yourselfers. Annie opened the bag and drew out the sporran.

"Ah, a sporran," Mike leaned closer to it. "Sealskin."

"Yes, that's what Alice thought it was," said Annie. She opened the clasp. "The items inside are what brought me here." She reached in to pull out the bands, setting them on the counter in a row. "Do you know what these are?"

Mike picked up one of the bands and examined it for a moment, silent. "Ayuh. These are ferrules, connector pieces for a bagpipe." Before he could say more, the front door of the store swung open and Reed Edwards, Stony Point's chief of police, filled the doorway. "Oh, excuse me, Annie," Mike said.

"Of course, Mike." Annie turned around to face Reed, looking up a fair distance to reach his face. "Good morning, Chief Edwards."

The chief was wearing jeans and a T-shirt, a far cry from his work uniform. Annie thought he looked even more like a lumberjack than usual.

"Morning, Annie. Everything quiet at Grey Gables these days?"

"Yes, except when Boots wants her food, or Alice plays a practical joke." Annie had had to call on Stony Point's small police department for assistance so many times she was almost embarrassed. Thankfully, Reed and his police officers had always kept her safe while maintaining general good humor.

"What can I get for you, Chief?" Mike asked.

Reed waved him off. "Just some things for softball field maintenance, Mike." The police chief came by his dark tan honestly. When he wasn't vigilantly watching over the citizens and property of Stony Point, he coached softball and spent time on the water. "Nothing I can't get for myself." He disappeared between two rows of shelves.

Mike and Annie focused their attention back on the ferrules. "Can you tell me anything about the engraving, Mike? Any idea what the significance of it might be?"

Mike's mustache quirked up on one side as he considered the symbol. "Bagpipe owners can have their ferrules engraved with anything that will fit on it, according to the skill level of the engraver." He set one of the ferrules on its side and gave it a little spin. "Whoever engraved these is a master. Sometimes a clan badge or symbol is used, or a military insignia or something significant to the pipe owner."

"Have you ever seen this bird and rose symbol before?" asked Annie.

Mike stopped the spin of the ferrule, picked it up and squinted at it. "No, I haven't. Wish I could be more help."

"Well, you gave me a place to start, Mike." Annie

scooped the ferrules into the sporran. "This is a long shot, but have you ever seen the design on the sporran clasp?" She closed the sporran and handed it to him.

Mike stared at the clasp. Before he could say anything, the back door of the store opened with a bang, forcing everyone's attention to the source of the noise. Trace Malone, his hair—a shade lighter than his sister's—almost covering his hazel eyes, grabbed the door as it bounced off the wall and shut it more gently than he'd opened it. "Sorry, Dad."

Mike set his lips into a straight thin line. "Clock battery needs replacing? Aisle 4. Back room needs work."

Trace glanced out the front window at his sister, his shoulders dropping. "OK, Dad." He knew better than to mumble. "Bye, Mrs. Dawson. Sorry I interrupted."

"Apology accepted, Trace." Annie smiled gently at the young man before she turned back to speak to his father. "So, have you seen anything like this?" She ran an index finger over the clasp.

Clearing his throat, Mike paused until his son had closed the door of the back room behind him and then smiled. "Believe it or not, that's one of the worst disciplines I could give that boy. He hates the back room, small with no windows and no way out except past me."

"Kailyn told me Trace stays outdoors as much as possible."

"Ayuh. That's why we nicknamed him Trace. Seems every time I'd ask where the boy was, someone would answer, 'Haven't seen a trace of him.' Then we'd find him outside somewhere, digging holes or climbing a fence or tree." Mike glanced out the window at Kailyn. "I've always hoped one of my children would want to work with me and then take over the store when I retire. I've finally accepted it isn't going to be Trace. Never crossed my mind it might be one of my daughters."

Annie held back from grinning as wide as she wanted to and commented discreetly, "Kailyn seems very comfortable here."

"She is," Mike agreed. "She's almost as fast at finding things as I am now." He pulled in a deep breath and pointed to the sporran. "Anyway, I haven't seen this design either. If I think of someone who might be able to help you, I'll be sure to let you know."

Annie tucked the sporran into her bag. "Thanks, Mike. I'd appreciate it. Say hello to Fiona for me. Tell her we need to get together and catch up."

"She'd like that." Mike went ahead and opened the door for her. "So long, Annie."

Kailyn was emptying the rubbish she had swept and collected into a trash can by the curb. "Have a good day, Mrs. Dawson."

"I plan to, Kailyn. You too." Annie paused, tilting her face to the warm sunshine. It was a perfect day for an iced coffee, The Cup & Saucer style. Across Oak Lane from the diner, the Stony Point Library caught her eyes. She considered popping in first to check the nonfiction section for Celtic design information, but the lure of a frosty java won. She stepped off the curb to cross the street at an angle toward the diner.

As Annie approached the door, a tall man in precisely ironed gray pants and a blue oxford shirt with sleeves rolled up to the elbow strode across Oak Lane. "Hello, Annie!" Ian Butler's call was as warm and cheerful as the August morning.

"Hi, Ian!" Annie paused to allow the mayor of Stony Point to catch up to her. "I feel for you, having to spend the day in your office. This might be the most gorgeous day of the year."

Ian grinned. "I did take Tartan out for a long walk along the shore early this morning." He opened the diner door and held it open for Annie. "And I sense another walk coming before dinner. Days like this are the best free advertisements for our fair town."

Annie gestured at the growing number of pedestrians strolling along Main Street before she stepped through the door. "The tourists do seem to be enjoying themselves. I just ran into Chief Edwards at Malone's. Apparently the softball field has been getting plenty of use too." She ran her gaze around the diner. "I don't see Peggy; maybe she's in the back." Annie enjoyed any chance to see her younger friend. As a quilter, Peggy was a member, along with Annie and Alice, of the town's Hook and Needle Club.

Ian waved her over to a booth by the window. "Peggy will be taking a couple days off. She tripped over a loose board on the dock and twisted her right wrist when she landed."

"Oh, no!" Annie exclaimed. Peggy Carson and her husband, Wally, were hard workers, but the economic downturn had brought difficulty to their small family, as it had to so many. The family could ill afford the loss of Peggy's income. "I'll check on Peggy before I head home. One handed cooking isn't any easier than one-handed waitressing, even with little Emily to help." She fixed her eyes on the mayor. "I do hope the dock gets repaired as soon as possible."

"The board has already been replaced," Ian assured her.

"As soon as Wally called me, I sent a crew over. We can't have our citizens or visitors hurt while enjoying the waterfront."

"I appreciate your diligence, Ian," said Annie. "I wonder how Lisa is going to handle the whole room during a tourist season shift?"

Ian smiled. "Here comes the answer to your question, I think."

Annie looked up to see Breck—the young man who usually bused tables—heading toward them with a pad clutched in his long fingers. He stopped, towering over them, his eyes shy. He asked in a voice that sounded as though he didn't use it very much, "What can I get for you … uh, Miss Annie, Mayor Butler?"

"Just an iced coffee for me, Breck," answered Annie. "How do you like waiting tables?"

Breck tossed his head to swing the tawny curls from his eyes and scribbled on the pad. After an extended pause he managed, "Won't be long."

"I'll have a regular coffee and an egg sandwich," Ian said. After Breck had scribbled and left, he turned his attention back to Annie. "Tartan and I went a little too far on our morning walk, and I had to skip breakfast to get to an early meeting on time."

"You didn't skip it," Annie chuckled. "You just postponed it a bit."

Ian leaned across the table and lowered his voice, his eyes mischievous. "Would that Charlotte was as good-natured about it. I think she would have rapped my knuckles with a ruler, if there'd been one handy. Perhaps her upcoming vacation will loosen her up again and bring back her smile." Charlotte Nash was Ian's executive assistant at City Hall. He settled back against the back of the booth. "So, tell me what you've been up to lately."

Annie paused as Breck served their beverages. "I have found myself, to my utter surprise, to be nurturing thriving gardens this summer," she bragged to Ian. "Most of my mornings are spent in my vegetables and flowers." She paused and lifted her project bag. "And … I'm sure this will be shocking to you … my attic has provided me with another mystery."

"Well, it's about time!" said Ian. "It's been a bit since the last one. If it's fitting in your project bag, it must be smaller than the last one."

Annie lifted the sporran out of the bag and opened the clasp to draw out the ferrules to show Ian. "This is why I came into town today, to find out more about this sporran. Mike just told me that these bands are ferrules—parts of a bagpipe. I don't remember Gram and Grandpa ever showing these to me or having a bagpipe. Why would they be in Grey Gables's attic?"

"May I?" After Annie's nod, Ian picked up first a ferrule and then the sporran. "I seem to remember one of your grandparents being from Scottish roots. I know these Celtic designs can be Scottish, Irish, or Welsh, but maybe that's the connection."

"Yes, Gram's family hailed from Scotland," Annie confirmed. "But I don't think this is connected with them, or I'm sure she would have shown it to me. Both of my grandparents loved telling me family stories, you know. But just to make sure, I'm going to check out the family names and see if I can find any connection to these symbols." She pointed to the clasp. "Do you know what that sprig is from?"

Ian examined the clasp and then nodded. "It's some type of juniper." He ran his hand along the sleek fur. "I know this is sealskin. Imports of sealskin to the U.S. have been banned for decades, so it's probably older than the ban."

"Another thing I can't figure out is why I found a sporran but no kilt, even after searching for hours with Alice, and ferrules but no bagpipes. How about the engraving on the ferrules; have you ever seen anything like it?" Annie took a sip of her iced coffee.

Ian pondered the bird and rose and shook his head. "No, I don't remember seeing anything like this." Breck sidled up to the table and slid the plate containing an egg sandwich in front of Ian. "Thanks, Breck." The young man gave the barest hint of a nod, which more resembled a muscle spasm, before turning aside to another table.

"I'm thinking of checking at the library for Scottish clan information, in case the connection is to Gram's family. Any ideas for other places where I might find some expert help?" Ian had often helped Annie solve the mysteries she so regularly stumbled upon—sometimes literally.

"Now let me think on it a minute," said Ian.

Annie smiled. "Eat your sandwich. Maybe the nourishment will spark an idea."

In response, Ian took a hearty bite, chewing thoroughly as he considered possibilities. His eyes brightened, and then he swallowed. "Hey, have you heard of the Maine Highland Games?" he asked. "It's held every August at the Topsham Fairgrounds. All kinds of vendors and demonstrators fill the lanes. You'll find a good deal of Scottish knowledge in one place."

"August? Do you know when in August?" asked Annie. "I might just cry if it was this past weekend."

Ian finished wiping his mouth with his napkin. "No tears needed. It's always on the third Saturday of August. Are you free that weekend?"

"I'm pretty sure I am," Annie answered, hoping she hadn't forgotten anything on her calendar at home. "How far is Topsham from here?"

"Right next door in Sagadahoc County," Ian said, setting his coffee cup down. "I'd be glad to take you. They have the best sheepdog trials around these parts, and I haven't had the chance to go the last few years."

"Are you thinking of breaking Tartan into another career?" Annie grinned.

"Now, that would be sure to give everyone some entertainment!" Ian laughed. "So, how about it?"

"I'd love to, just let me check my calendar to make sure I haven't forgotten anything. May I call you later to confirm?" Annie sipped the last few drops of her iced coffee, refreshed by both the beverage and the conversation.

"Of course you can," said Ian. His voice slipped into his "official" voice. "As mayor, I'm always pleased to hear from my constituents, especially when said constituent is a pretty Texas transplant with a penchant for mysteries and a talent for cooking."

A few minutes later the couple said goodbye and departed to go their separate ways, one to City Hall and the other back to Grey Gables.

— 4 —

"I can't believe you refused to get up early enough for us to walk downtown." Annie glanced sideways at Alice from the driver's seat of her car on Tuesday morning. "It won't be long before this perfect weather is just a memory."

"I told you August is my semi-vacation month," Alice argued, with a chuckle hiding behind her words. "Early rising would totally ruin the whole concept. I promise to take a good long jaunt after the meeting, if it will make you happy."

Annie turned left from Oak Lane to Main Street, slowing to look for a parking space near A Stitch in Time, Stony Point's needlecraft shop and meeting place for the Hook and Needle Club. "Early rising? The meeting's at eleven o'clock! Are you sure you want to go with Ian and me to the Highland Games? We're leaving at eight o'clock in the morning, sharp. It might ruin your semi-vacation month."

As usual, Stella Brickson had already arrived, her white Lincoln parked right in front of the shop door with her driver, Jason, standing beside it. He waved as Annie pulled into the parking space behind him.

As she opened her door, Alice answered her friend. "I think an event that I've never attended and that happens only once a year is sufficient motivation for getting up so horribly early."

"Well, thank the Lord for *that*," Annie said. She grinned at Alice and exited the car. "Good morning, Jason."

"Hello, Annie. Alice." Seven years of life in Maine had done nothing to alter the man's strong New York accent. Annie supposed after seven years, she would still have plenty of the Lone Star state in her voice. "Great baseball weather we're having."

"Shall we tell Stella you'll be at the Yankees game, should she need you?" Alice asked, batting her eyelashes outrageously at him.

Jason pointed a curled-up sports section of the *New York Times* at her. "Don't tempt me, Alice. Don't tempt me."

At that, Alice opened the door of the shop and Annie followed her inside so they wouldn't miss the start of the meeting.

A Stitch in Time had grown a reputation in the nearby counties for being a place filled with inspiration and the supplies to make those inspirations real. More and more customers had found their way there, and it was particularly busy during tourist season when folks were looking for something to occupy themselves during long rides, whether in a car, plane, or train. But Annie still found herself a little surprised to see several people she'd never seen on a Tuesday morning.

The owner, Mary Beth Brock, stood behind the cash register ringing up a pile of yarns and pattern books. Excusing herself to the customer, she called out. "Hi, Annie and Alice! I'll be there in just a few minutes. Please let the others know."

"We will, Mary Beth," said Annie. "Don't rush; we all have plenty to work on, I'm sure." She turned to Alice as they walked to the familiar circle of chairs where the Hook and Needle Club meetings took place.

"Or a mystery to talk about," Alice whispered. "You did bring the sporran, didn't you?"

Annie nodded before addressing the other members of the club. "Good morning, Stella and Gwen. Oh, and Kate," she added the last as the door to the back storage room opened to reveal the Mary Beth's shop assistant and crocheter extraordinaire.

"Hi, everyone," Kate greeted them. "I'm going to go relieve Mary Beth from helping customers so she can get the meeting started. I'm close enough that I won't miss much."

"Good," said Alice. "You always come up with such fun designs. Even though I don't crochet, I'm still inspired by them."

"Thanks, Alice." Kate paused on her way to take over for Mary Beth. "Even if the shop stays too busy, you'll get to see an example of my latest design. Mary Beth will be showing it to everyone."

"I'm going to miss seeing Peggy today," said Gwendolyn Palmer, wife of the president of Stony Point Savings Bank and an avid knitter.

"Well now, you don't have to go doing that, Gwen." Peggy sashayed into the meeting, her right hand bandaged tightly and her daughter Emily by her side. "Em and I would go bonkers sitting around home all day with Wally working extra hours this week."

Stella looked up from her knitting, her fingers not slowing at all, and gifted Peggy's young daughter with a smile. "Emily, you are old enough to begin learning a needlecraft. Do you have a favorite type?"

Unlike a fair amount of adults who were faced with Stella's scrutiny, Emily was comfortable conversing with the octogenarian widow. "I don't know, Mrs. Brickson. I kinda like them all."

"Perhaps, then, your goal should be to decide which one to learn first," said Stella.

"Maybe you can teach me to knit," Emily said. "Can—I mean—may I sit next to you and watch you today, Mrs. Brickson?" Emily stood at the seat next to Stella, while the ladies around the room kept their smiles restricted to their minds.

Stella fixed her eyes on the eight-year-old, who bobbed up and down from toe to heel, heel to toe, as she waited for the answer. "You may sit and watch, Emily, but no touching, mind you. This delicate, light yarn will show the smallest of smudges."

Emily held up both hands, as if in surrender. "No touching, I promise. I'll sit on my hands if I have to."

"Good thing you're not the one who tripped on the dock," Peggy said with a wry grin as she took a seat between Gwen and Alice. Her daughter laughed and plopped herself down next to Stella.

Mary Beth strode past the group. "I'll be right there!" she explained as she continued to the shop's small office. A short minute later she re-emerged with something colorful in her left hand. "Before we share our individual projects today, I have a request to pass on from Carla Calloway at the animal shelter. She needs some immediate help."

"What's up?" Alice asked, couching a line of tiny dark gray stitches over a curve of metallic silver thread. The other women, and Emily, looked up from their work to give the shop owner their full attention.

"The animal shelter has a challenge on its hands. There is a battery chicken house outside of town and inspectors found the hens to be horribly malnourished. Over a hundred hens have been rescued. They have lost most of their feathers and keep pecking at the few they have left."

Emily stuck out her bottom lip. "Did the police get the bad guys who were so mean to those chickens?"

"Yes. I did hear those involved with the farm have all been charged with animal cruelty," answered Mary Beth, "and Carla is trying very hard to help the hens heal. But she needs the help of Stony Point knitters and crocheters." She unfolded the crocheted piece in her hand, revealing a small sweater. "Kate worked with Carla to design a sweater for the hens to protect the remaining feathers until the others have grown back. I also have a knitting pattern to share." She handed the sweater to Annie to pass around the circle.

"I saw a news report on something like this," Alice interjected. "In England, a knitting club made sweaters for battery hens from a similar farm there."

"Why are they called battery hens, Alice?" Annie asked.

"Because they are placed in very small cages—some so small the hens can't even turn around," Alice explained. "They are then put in long rows—called batteries—because that produces the most eggs for the least amount of space and chicken feed. It's not illegal in the United States—as far as I know—but it sure sounds inhumane to me."

"If I *had* to hurt my hand, I guess this was a good time," said Peggy. "Quilting doesn't really work for chicken sweaters. So I'll just cheer the rest of you on."

Annie turned the sweater over in her hands, noting the stitch types used. "We should be able to knock these out pretty fast. Kate's design looks simple yet effective. I'll get started right away. I'm not making anything that can't be set aside for a little while." She passed the sweater over to Gwen.

"My needles are yours, Mary Beth, for as long as it takes," said Gwen, setting her needles and scarf in her lap and examining the sweater. "I'm thankful the authorities put a stop to it. The people of Stony Point will not put up with animal abuse in our community!"

Stella nodded as her hands continued to churn out stitches. "I have a few friends who are knitters and crocheters, but who aren't able to attend our meetings. Do you have extra copies of the patterns, Mary Beth? I'd be glad to recruit more help."

"I knew I could count on all of you," said Mary Beth. "There are plenty of copies to share."

"What can I do?" Emily asked. "I can't knit or crochet yet."

The earnest look on the young girl's face tugged at the shop owner's heart. "Emily, as you probably saw when you and your mother came in, business is hopping. I could really use help in collecting and keeping count of the completed sweaters. Would you be willing to take that important job off my hands?"

Emily bounced in her seat. "I can do it, Miss Mary Beth!"

"Wonderful, Emily. I've got something for you." Mary Beth walked over to the storage room and disappeared for a moment, returning with a large red fabric bag emblazoned with *A Stitch in Time*. "When this is filled with sweaters, return it to me along with the number of sweaters inside it, and I will take them to Miss Calloway."

Emily took the bag and hugged it to her chest. "You can count on me."

"Hmmm." Alice's eyes narrowed in mock concentration. "Emily's in charge of sweater inventory; Peggy's the project cheerleader. What is this cross-stitcher going to do?" She paused, a mischievous smile began in her eyes and spread. "Besides helping Annie with her new mystery, that is."

Everyone sat up a little straighter and heads swiveled in unison like a parade band commanded to "dress center"—the center being Annie.

"Now, don't just sit there," Peggy said, waving her bandaged hand. "Spill it! And please tell us you brought something besides yarn in your bag?"

Annie chuckled as everyone leaned toward her and nodded their agreement with Peggy. Even Stella appeared interested, although the speedy clicking of her needles never slowed. "Good thing for me my discovery doesn't weigh a hundred pounds," Annie said. She reached into her project bag and drew out the sporran. "I thought mice had invaded my attic again ... but it turned out to be a sporran instead."

"What's a sporran?" asked Emily.

"A sporran is a pouch that serves like a pocket for a kilt," Stella answered her young friend.

Alice anticipated Emily's next question. "And a kilt is a traditional Scottish garment for men and boys. It looks like a knee-length pleated skirt."

"I don't think my daddy would want to be Scottish and wear a skirt." Emily shook her head slowly.

"Annie, some of your family was from Scotland, if I remember correctly," said Gwen. "How is the sporran a mystery?"

Annie smiled at her friend whose knowledge of Stony Point's family lines was quite extensive. "Yes, you're right, Gwen. Gram's family *was* from Scotland. But you know what storytellers my grandparents were. They were always telling me one yarn or another about our ancestors and showing me family heirlooms. Not once during my childhood did they show me this or any other sporran. I find that odd enough to be intrigued."

"Show them what's inside," Alice prompted.

Annie opened the clasp and took out the ferrules. "These ferrules are from bagpipes. Does anyone remember ever seeing my grandparents with a bagpipe?" She walked around the circle with the ferrules on the palm of her right hand, offering everyone a closer look. Aware that Stella had known Annie's grandparents since her teens, Annie was particularly interested in her reaction.

The group was quiet for a moment as each person besides Annie and Alice examined the engravings on the ferrules. Then Emily whispered, "This is soooo cool!"

Stella handed a ferrule back to Annie. "Obviously, the engraver is a master silversmith. This is truly elegant work. I must say, I do not remember Charles or Betsy ever displaying or playing a bagpipe. Of course, I did live in New York for all those years."

Gwen jumped in, "But I was in town during those years, Stella, and I never saw Annie's grandparents with a set of bagpipes." She smiled in remembrance. "Like Annie, I can't imagine them not sharing them with the community, if they had them. They shared everything else—their cross-stitch, woodworking, gardening wisdom, animal knowledge, humor, baking, and stories. I understand, Annie."

"Annie and I searched around Grey Gables for hours looking for a kilt to go with the sporran," added Alice. "Not a single thread of kilt did we find."

Peggy rolled a ferrule between the thumb and index finger of her uninjured hand, anticipation brightening her face. "So, what's the next move?"

"The mayor gave me a good idea," Annie answered. "He suggested I might find some helpful information at the Maine Highland Games. And I only have to wait until the eighteenth!"

"Ah yes," Alice said, "Ian was good enough to offer the fair maiden a hand, drive her all the way there and spend a day in her company." Alice faked a martyr's sigh. "And I only have to lose hours of beauty sleep to go with her and keep her and Ian out of trouble."

"Thankfully, you have some beauty to spare," quipped Annie, blushing a bit about Alice's references to Ian. "Does anyone else want to come with us?"

Peggy fidgeted in her chair, reminding the others of her daughter. "I went to the Games once years ago. It's so much fun. And the dancing!"

Emily popped out of her chair and went to her mother. "Can we go? Please? I want to see the dancers!" Besides her parents, Emily loved dancing more than anything else in her young life. She stared at Peggy, pleading with her eyes.

"I'll talk to Daddy about it," Peggy promised her little ballerina. "It sure would be nice to have a fun family day, as long as it's not too expensive."

"There's no entrance fee," Annie told her, "so I hope you will be able to join us."

Gwen sighed and ran her hand lightly over her neat chignon. "I'll be gone that weekend at some boring bank event." She leaned toward her friends and lowered her voice. "They mean well, I'm sure, but some of these spouse events they plan are real snoozers."

The group chuckled sympathetically, and Alice assured her, "We'll make sure to tell you every detail, Gwen. Ian's going too, and you know how observant he is."

As one, the other women murmured "ohhhh!" and smiled knowingly. Blushing, Annie decided it was time to buy her yarn and get to work on the chicken sweaters.

5

A bit over a fortnight later, Alice opened the door of her carriage house to Ian's knock with the full intention of surprising him with an energetic greeting. Instead, a wide yawn escaped in place of the hearty "Good morning" she had planned.

She clapped a hand over her mouth, and Ian grinned and said, "And good morning to you too, Alice. Would you mind a short stop at The Cup & Saucer for coffee before we head out of town?"

"If you insist," she answered wryly, closing the door behind her and locking the deadbolt. "Haven't you been up for at least two hours, like Annie?" She gestured toward the car where her best friend sat in the front passenger seat.

"Well, yes, now that you mention it," Ian said as he opened the back car door for Alice. "But Tartan will be home alone again for the day, so I took him on a good long constitutional—a bit longer than I had anticipated, so coffee had to wait."

"Your eyes *are* open," Annie observed when Alice slid into the seat behind Ian. "Good for you."

Stifling another yawn, smaller than the last, Alice replied, "Very funny, Little Miss Sunrise. We'll see who has more energy by the end of the day."

"The Games end at five o'clock. I think even I can stay

lively until then," Annie quipped, even though she had been in the garden as soon as the sun had sent enough light to distinguish between weed and vegetable.

Ian put the car into reverse and backed out of the carriage house driveway. "After a quick stop for coffee we'll all have plenty of vigor to spare. Watch out, Scottish clans of the Highland Games!" he said.

A few minutes later Ian maneuvered his car into a parking space near the diner. "Three coffees to go?" he asked to confirm. Annie nodded, smiling and Alice blurted, "Absolutely! But you two might need some too." With a laugh, Ian exited the car and strode across the sidewalk to disappear into the building.

Annie gazed out the window at the quiet street. The fish and lobster boats had been on the Gulf of Maine for hours, but the tourists had not yet filled the walkways to explore the quaint village. A lone woman in jeans and a T-shirt walking briskly toward them caught Annie's eyes.

"Hi, Carla!" Annie rolled down the car window and called to the veterinarian and head of the animal shelter. "How are the hens doing?" She had spent the better part of the previous two weeks crocheting chicken sweaters in yellow, green, and blue yarn.

"Could be better," Carla answered in her typical clipped manner. "Could be worse." At the age of sixty-plus, she didn't see the need for wasting time on what she saw as superfluous chatter.

"Have you been able to find homes for them?" Alice asked.

"A couple of farmers have stepped up, but we need one

or two more," Carla answered. She fixed her dagger eyes on Annie. "The sweaters seem to be helping."

Annie wasn't sure, but it seemed to her she'd just heard a positive statement from the crusty woman, sadly nicknamed "Carla Callous" by someone in Stony Point. "I'm glad to hear it," Annie said. "Let us know if you need any more."

Carla jerked her chin down and up in response and continued on her way.

Alice's eyes followed the woman's staccato pace until she disappeared around the corner. "Carla's as different from your grandpa as a person can be, but there's no denying she's as strong an advocate for animals as he was."

"It would have been interesting to watch them interact, I'm sure," Annie said, picturing the two veterinarians in conversation. That brought a smile to her face.

Alice smiled too, but not because of Annie's words. She had just noticed the beverage carrier in Ian's hands as he came through The Cup & Saucer door, the one with two medium and two large coffee cups. "Now there's a mayor who knows how to serve his constituents."

Annie's head swiveled around to look, and then a laugh followed. "Yes," she said. "Yes, he does. I might consider voting for him when election day comes around. He'll be running on the 'More Coffee for Every Cup' platform."

"I'd be willing to hand out fliers for that campaign," Alice practically cooed as Ian opened the back door.

The mayor grinned and lifted one of the medium cups out of the carrier and presented it to Alice. A raised eyebrow replaced the woman's coo. "It's not nice to play a joke before caffeine has been administered."

Ian bobbed his head and set the smaller cup back into the carrier. "How could I forget? That's one of the first rules I learned while preparing for government work." He held out a large cup. "My apologies, Alice."

"If that second large cup is also for me, then apology accepted." Alice flicked the cover flap up with a thumb and breathed in the strong brew. "Aaaah! The fog is already lifting."

Ian gifted Alice with the second large cup and took his place behind the wheel of his sedan, placing the remaining two cups in the holders between Annie and him. After tucking the carrier out of sight in the glove compartment, he started the engine, and craning his head, pulled out of the parking space. "Topsham Fairgrounds, here we come!"

Alice lowered her coffee cup after a good deep draught. "Annie, I've been thinking. Did you bring the sporran and the ferrules with you? I realized it might not be the safest thing to do with the crowds."

"I thought about that too," her friend replied. "So, I took some photos and printed them out." She reached into her summer handbag and pulled out several pages. "These should be enough to show vendors, don't you think?" She handed the photos back to Alice.

Alice looked through them. "These should work fine. You've taken them from different angles so it's almost as good as having the sporran with you." She dangled the pages over the seat so Annie could put them back in her bag.

"I did bring one of the ferrules," added Annie. "But I left the others tucked away in Grey Gables with Boots as watch cat."

"I hope you fed Boots well for her assignment," joked Ian as he turned off Main Street to head south.

The two women snorted simultaneously. "It's Boots we're talking about here," Annie reminded him. "Of course I did."

Alice chimed in. "Daring to leave Boots without her kibble is like denying Garfield his lasagna. Dangerous."

"I stand ... uh, sit, corrected." Ian smiled, realizing just how much he was looking forward to spending the entire day with the two vivacious friends.

The ride to Topsham flew by on the speedy wings of conversation and wit. They were all taken by surprise when the sign for the turnoff to the fairgrounds appeared.

"Where are we meeting the Carsons?" Alice asked as Ian slowly drove by the lines of parked vehicles looking for an open spot.

"Wally told me to call him when we're at the main parade field so they can meet us there." Ian paused as he waited for a couple to walk past in front of the empty space he intended to fill. "They usually have big tents with different-color stripes around the field. If we find one with a unique color, it'll make it easier for them to find us." The way cleared, he pulled into the space and parked.

Annie exited the car, digging into her bag to retrieve a periwinkle blue brimmed hat. As she adjusted the hat over her forehead so she had just enough to shade her eyes from the sun without blocking her vision, she looked around. "And what direction would the parade field be?"

Ian was gazing at Annie, admiring how the color of her hat made her eyes appear even greener. He paused in answering long enough to draw the attention of Alice, who allowed a shadow of a smile to cross her lips. Ignoring Alice's expression, Ian gestured ahead of them and to the left. "This way, ladies. Just let me grab the chairs." He popped open the trunk with his key and ducked behind it to retrieve the chairs.

Alice pulled a Red Sox baseball cap out of her jeans pocket and settled it on her head, drawing her high auburn ponytail through the hole in the back while laughing to herself that the mayor would be much less enamored with her style choice. But since she had never been able to feel anything but a warm friendship for Ian, she was fine with that.

At the entrance to the Highland Games, Ian obtained brochures of the event for each of them. He glanced at his watch. "We have plenty of time to find a good vantage point for the parade of bands. Let's check out the tents." The three wove through the groups of people milling around the smaller tents near the entrance. Once they reached the perimeter of the large level main field, they stopped to take in the scene before them. Tall trees wearing their summer green lushness bordered the field, making a fine backdrop for the festivities.

"The tents look so cheery against the green trees," Annie said. "I see three yellow-stripe tents, two green-stripes, and one blue-stripe over there." She pointed to the blue tent positioned near the center of the field lengthwise. "Anyone see another blue-stripe tent?"

After a minute of scanning around the whole field, Alice shook her head. "I don't."

"Neither do I," agreed Ian, "and it's near the center of

the field, making it a great vantage point. Let's meet the Carsons there."

As they made their way toward the blue-stripe tent, the mayor called Wally to tell him where they would meet. "Wally's just parked," he informed Annie and Alice after returning his phone to its case attached to his belt. "They won't be long."

When they arrived at the blue-stripe tent, a lot of people had already set out chairs behind the colorful flagged barrier, but there was still room for the Stony Point contingent. Ever the gentleman, Ian opened the camp chairs and made sure the two women were comfortable; then he strolled back and forth over the adjacent square of grass to keep it free for the Carsons.

Annie's eyes sparkled as she watched the activity around her and felt the cooling breeze flow across the field to caress her. "I still can't get over the difference between Maine and Texas Augusts," she said. "There was no way I would go to an all-day outdoor event in August back home. OK, maybe I would go, if I had to, but I wouldn't enjoy it." She leaned back in her chair with a happy sigh. "Here I can people-watch all I want without sweating; I like that."

Alice looked sideways in Ian's direction. "I think Ian wants to *person*-watch." She leaned closer to Annie and dropped her voice. "Did you notice how he looked at you while you were putting on your hat? Rarely is our mayor so entranced by headgear."

Annie opened her mouth to deny Alice's observation, something she'd begun to do instinctively over the prior few months, but she saw the Carsons making their way toward them. "Oh, there they are." She waved vigorously at the parents and daughter.

Peggy had slung a large bag stuffed with an old quilt from her shoulder, her wrist now free of any bandaging. Alice called out to them, "Come stake your claim. Ian's been working hard to keep that patch clear of squatters."

"Thanks, Mr. Mayor," Peggy said as she approached Ian. "The crowds are growing fast." She lowered the bag to the ground and pulled the quilt free to spread it next to Ian's chair. "Even Em won't have any trouble seeing everything from here."

Emily jumped up and down, pointing across the field. "Mom, look! All those people are in skirts, I mean, kilts." She ran over to her father, who was talking to Ian. "Look, Daddy! Those are the kilts I was telling you about. Would you ever wear one?"

Annie consulted her brochure. "Wally, if you and Ian can each buy a kilt before noon you could enter the Bonnie Knees contest."

The face of the quiet handyman flushed, but he laughed at the suggestion. "Annie, you're one of my best customers, along with Ian, but there's no way you could get me in one of those things. No matter what fancy word you use, it's still a skirt."

"I guess it's a good thing you're not Scottish then," Peggy said, straightening a corner of the blanket and sitting down. She looked across the field to see the bands arranged in neat lines. "Looks like it's starting soon." She patted the blanket beside her. "Come relax after your busy week."

"Do I have to sit?" asked Emily. "Can't I just stand

right here?" The ride from Stony Point had been more than enough sitting for the young girl.

Understanding, Peggy looked behind them to make sure her daughter wouldn't be blocking the view of other people. "It's all right, as long as you don't forget and dance in front of folks so they can't see."

"I won't," the girl promised. She reached down to hug her mother and then stood beside the blanket swaying like a young sapling in the breeze. "Here they come!" she squealed as the stewards gave the signal and the first bagpipes-and-drum band marched onto the fields playing *God Bless America*, led by three flagmen.

It had been several years since Annie had heard bagpipes being played. As the following bands joined the first, and the sound swelled, her attention was captured by the unique sound. She reached into her bag and fingered the solitary ferrule. Had any of her family members played the haunting instrument?

"They have funny shoes," Emily commented, holding back a giggle. "Or are they funny boots?"

"They're called spats, Emily," answered Ian. "They are made from thick canvas, usually, and attached over boots or shoes."

Emily's eyes were trained on the bands, but her slim body kept moving to the rhythm of the drums. "Spats. I like that word. Snazzy spats." She did giggle that time. A moment later she gasped and pointed to the band that had just stepped on the field. "Look at the band in red and black. See that kid? He looks about my age!"

Wally shielded his eyes with a hand as he peered at the

band. "He sure does, Em." They all watched as the pint-sized piper moved smoothly across the field in perfect step with the rest of the band.

"He's got a good sense of timing, you can tell," said Annie. "I wonder how heavy those bagpipes are. Do you know, Alice?"

Alice shook her head. "Not really. I've never held one, but I suspect they come in different weights, especially since they can be made from different types of wood and with plastic or metal parts."

"Sounds like a good question to ask those vendors you're planning to visit, Annie," Ian suggested.

A gust of breeze threatened to snatch Annie's hat off her head. She grabbed it just in time and settled it more snuggly. "If I remember, I'll ask. Or maybe Alice and Peggy can do that while I concentrate on the sporran and ferrules."

"I love watching the guys with the bass drums," Peggy declared. "Em, see how they twirl the mallets in between the beats?"

Having lost sight of the boy when the band turned to position themselves behind an earlier band, Em moved her attention to the drummers of a band closer to where they were sitting. "I wonder if they ever hit themselves with all that twirling and whirling."

"The beaters look kinda puffy to me," said Wally. "That might soften the blow if they mess up."

Emily laughed at that before turning her attention back to the finale, as all the bands played *Scotland the Brave* and then marched smartly off the field.

Alice nudged Annie as the bands turned about-face and moved away from them. "Look at all those sporrans out there. Never thought about them being worn in the back, but it makes sense with the pipes and drums. Ian's suggestion to come here for information was spot on."

Annie smiled over at Ian. "Well, you know our mayor, Alice. He's always one to serve. We may have to treat him to a haggis lunch."

"What's haggis?" asked Emily.

Ian pictured the traditional Scottish savory pudding that includes some of the internal organs of sheep. He clasped the shoulder of his young friend. "Trust me, Em," he said, "you don't want to know. Not before you've had lunch, anyway."

6

Peggy folded the Carsons' quilt and tucked it into her bag. "What should we do next?"

"I'd really like to start checking with the vendors about the sporran and ferrule," said Annie. "But I hate for y'all to feel like you have to follow me around."

Alice intertwined her arm with Annie's. "You know how much I enjoy poking around all kinds of shops, so I'm following you around voluntarily. Besides, I'm as curious about all this as you are."

"Me too," Peggy chimed in. "As long as we can see some of the dancing, I'd rather keep together." She paused and glanced sideways at her husband, who was good-natured but not much for shopping. "But Wally and Ian might want to do something else."

Wally ran a hand through his hair. "Well, we won't need the chairs or quilt until the afternoon competitions, so Ian and I could take them back to the car and then … " he paused, thinking.

Ian consulted the brochure. "Wally, are you interested in seeing any of the livestock? I have to admit I have a soft spot for Highland cattle. Their hair is as pretty as Alice's—almost." Wally agreed with Ian's suggestion as the friends chuckled.

"You know what I say to my hair stylist every time I

go, right?" said Alice. "Please make my hair shine like a Highland cow!"

When the laughter had died down, Annie asked, "Does everyone want to see the falconry demonstration? If you do, we could meet there at, say, ten thirty." Her friends all showed enthusiasm for the idea, and the two groups parted, Emily giving Wally a quick hug before joining her mother for the walk to the vendor tents.

The first vendor the ladies found sported the sign, "MacTavish, Pipemaker." Inside the white tent, tables and portable shelving displayed a variety of full bagpipes, parts, and maintenance items, such as hemp and wax. There were also instruction books, DVDs, and computer programs.

Looking around, Emily noticed something that looked familiar to her. "Hey, they've got recorders here." She pointed at some long pieces, some plastic, and others made of wood. After bending over to get a closer look, she muttered, "These look a little weird, though."

"Well, lassie, that's because they're not recorders," said a man with light brown hair tending toward gray and gray eyes tending toward humor. "You're looking at chanters, you are."

Emily's blue eyes widened as she gazed up into the man's face. "I've never heard of a chanter."

"Why, it's a very important part of a bagpipe," the man said as he picked up one of the instruments made of dark wood, flared on one end. "This one is made of blackwood, and if you tried to play one of these on a bagpipe, you'd probably end up fainting before getting a single note out." He set the chanter down in its place and picked up a narrower plastic version. "This is where a new piper needs to start, with a practice chanter. Learning to play the full bagpipes with bag and four reeds is a lot easier once you've mastered the practice chanter." He looked at the adults and grinned. "It also causes less pain for the people and dogs within a mile of the new player."

Emily looked from the practice chanter to the full bagpipes propped up on a nearby table. "Wow, that boy in the band this morning must have started practicing when he was a baby!"

"What colors was he wearing?" the man asked.

"Red and black."

"You must be talking about Colby. He's a rare one. I've only known one other piper who played as well so young." For a brief instance the merry eyes of the man dimmed, but he gave a slight shake of his head and then addressed Emily's companions. "Is there anything I can help you find?"

Peggy and Alice looked at Annie, who reached into her bag for the ferrule. "There might be," Annie said, showing the man the ferrule. "I found eight of these, with no bagpipe, in the house my grandparents used to own. I was wondering if you might be able to tell me anything about the engraving, whether it's from a particular clan or family."

The man reached out a hand, and asked, "May I?" Annie placed the piece in his hand. "You have eight of them, you say? That's one short of a complete set." He took a pair of glasses out of his shirt pocket, donned them, and examined the mystery ferrule. "Sterling silver, excellent craftmanship." He paused and sighed. "Unfortunately, I don't know of any clan with that crest." He handed the ferrule back to Annie. "But there are several tartan and clan tents where you will find people to help you look for clan crests and badges."

"Thank you, Mr. … " Annie started.

"MacTavish—like the sign says," the pipemaker said. "I hope you will come back and see me, if you ever decide to learn piping." He chuffed Emily gently under the chin. "Especially you, lassie. And come back next year to see young Colby play again. He'll be a whole year better."

Emily bobbed her head. "I will, if Mom and Daddy bring me. Bye, Mr. MacTavish!"

As Emily and the women left, Mr. MacTavish stood staring after them, deep in thought.

The women wove between the tents, seeking out more bagpipe or music vendors. Annie showed the ferrule to three more pipe experts, all of whom showed interest in the quality of the piece and design. None of them, however, could tell her anything about the hawk-and-rose design.

After they thanked the last vendor, Peggy stopped her friends outside the tent. "You know I'm all for clue hunting," she said, "but if we don't do the next part of the search more quickly, we won't make it through all the vendors before we're supposed to meet Wally and Ian. I suggest we split up."

Alice looked at her watch. "Hmmm, I see what you mean. We've passed several tartan and clan tents, so I agree with your suggestion, Peggy."

"I do, also," said Annie. "Em, will you help your mom look for two things, the hawk-and-rose symbol and—" she pulled the photos of the sporran out of her bag and showed them to the young girl, "see the design on the clasp? The sprig is juniper. If we can find out what clan is associated with juniper, it might help us solve the mystery." Then she handed two of the photos to Peggy. "Take these with you."

"And call or text us if you find anything," Alice told her. "Immediately!"

Peggy snorted to beat any Highland cow. "As if you had to tell me that!" She pointed to the row of tents opposite from where they were standing. "Em and I will take that side, and you two take this one."

"Sounds good," agreed Annie. "If we don't find anything before 10:25, then let's meet at MacTavish's and go meet the guys."

Peggy saluted, and with a "Happy hunting!" she and Em went on their way. The first tent they came to, Dress to Kilt, radiated with color. Clan tartans draped racks along the canvas walls, looking like mini waterfalls. Spinning displays of kilt pins and accessories flanked the entrance.

"Em, you look at those pins," Peggy said, pointing her daughter to the display just across the entrance from where they were standing. "I'll check the ones over here." Excited to be a part of the sleuthing, Emily danced over to fulfill her assignment.

As mother and daughter concentrated on the pin designs, they didn't notice the slim teenager in a dark kilt and black shirt come through the entrance until he started fiddling. Then they peered around the two displays to watch the young musician serenade the girl behind a table, who blushed delicately under the freckles that sprinkled her pale but lovely face.

He ended with a flourish and held out his fiddle and

bow in supplication, layers of dark hair almost covering his eyes. "Will fiddle for kilt pin," he said.

Emily clapped her hand over her mouth, and Peggy ducked slightly behind the display to hide her smile.

"My parents would never let me come back next year if I started bartering away inventory on entertainment, Eli." The girl's voice started out prim, like she was channeling a schoolmarm from the Victorian era. Then the corners of her mouth turned up, and her eyes softened. "Even if the fiddler is cute when he plays."

The fiddler shifted one foot forward and gestured at his kilt with his bow. "Aw, Linley, I lost my kilt pin, and now I'll have to keep flashing my thighs at everyone."

"You may not thank me for it, but they will." Linley's smile widened into cheekiness. "But, maybe … ." The girl turned and poked her head through a gap in the back wall of the tent, looking left and then right to make sure her parents weren't nearby. "I could loan you a pin until the end of the day. You'll have to bring it back, or I'm in deep trouble when they do inventory. You wouldn't want that, would you?"

Eli stepped as close to the girl as he could get with the table between them and leaned over the obstacle, speaking in a low voice. "I'd never want trouble for you. But won't your parents be here at the end of the day, loading up stuff?"

"Yeah, probably." Linley gave the young man a look that had Peggy suddenly feeling like an intruder. She suddenly was reminded of when she first fell for Wally. "I guess we'll just have to meet somewhere away from the tent."

Eli gazed into the girl's eyes. "Can you meet me at the Harper's building? I'll be helping my aunt pack up, but I can get away for a few minutes." His expression communicated how much he wished it could be longer.

A woman in khaki Bermuda shorts and a shirt sprinkled with blue and red lobsters broke into the aura of blooming love in the tent to look around. Linley whispered, "OK," and then looked down at the kilt pins on the table. Selecting one, she slipped it into a small paper bag. Eli transferred his bow into the same hand as his fiddle and held out his hand. The girl laid the bag on his palm, delaying long enough to give the musician a chance to close his fingers briefly around hers.

The woman in the Bermuda shorts stepped up to the table and addressed the girl, "Do you have any pins with the Cross of St. Andrew?" With a wink, Eli released Linley's hand and slipped from the shop, while the object of his affection saw to the needs of the customer.

"Yes, we have several different pins." As the girl pointed them out to the woman, Peggy and Emily left the displays by the entrance and perused the pins on the table, but they saw no hawk-and-rose or juniper sprigs.

"The pins here are pretty, Mom, but I don't see anything like the pictures," Emily said to Peggy.

"On to the next place we go, then." Peggy took her daughter's hand, and they left the tent. "I can't wait to tell Annie and Alice about Eli and Linley. They were so sweet."

Emily giggled, "They were all googly-eyed."

"Now we have to look really fast in these other tents." Peggy pointed to a blue tent a few tents ahead of them. "Let's try that one next."

While mother and daughter explored their side of the tents, Annie and Alice ducked inside the tent of a vendor of clan tartans and crests. The riotous colors gave the portable room a cheerful atmosphere, which matched the energy of the entire Highland Games and kept the two women from feeling discouraged in their search. Against one wall stood several collections of matted clan crests and badges, ready for framing.

"We can each start at an end and work our way in," suggested Alice.

"Works for me," Annie agreed and moved to the far end of the wall. "Hopefully, this place will give us more info to go on than Mr. MacTavish did."

Alice started flipping through the matted and plastic-covered prints, which began alphabetically with Abercromby. "He seemed like a nice guy, though. I suspect he'd be a hoot at a Robbie Burns Dinner."

"Have you ever been to a Burns Dinner?" Annie asked as she looked at the first clan at her end, Young. The badge for that clan was yew and the crest looked nothing like the hawk and rose on the ferrule.

"Well, no," Alice admitted. "But I've heard about them. The same group that helps put on the Highland Games hosts a dinner in Portland to celebrate Robert Burns's birthday." She moved swiftly past the first several clans, not seeing anything either. "You know, since you do have Scottish roots in your family, we should think about going to one some year."

"Maybe," Annie began to answer. "Hey! I found a juniper! It's the badge for clan Ross." She lifted out the print to examine it closer. "But there's no hawk or rose in the crest." She returned the print to its place and pulled a small notepad from her purse, jotting down the name.

Spurred on by the find, the two women stopped the chatter and picked up the pace of their search. Soon, it was Alice's turn for discovery. "Here's another juniper badge! It's for clan Gunn. Hmmm, no hawk and rose here either."

Annie added "Gunn" to her list, and within a few minutes, they had met in the middle and added three more clan names—MacLeod, Murray, and Nicolson.

"Well, we've narrowed down considerably the possible name for the owner of the sporran," said Alice. "Not a bad half-morning's work."

Annie was staring at her list. "But we don't know if the owner was a man or woman. It may be a family heirloom passed down to a daughter. Likely, a daughter would marry and not be a Ross, Gunn, MacLeod, Murray, or Nicolson anymore. The owner could now be a Perez or Svingli for all we know."

"We've had less to go on with other mysteries, Annie," Alice reminded her friend. "Somehow, a pathway always manages to open up. It's a start."

Annie nodded, thankful for her friend's perspective. "Yes, it is. And we still have plenty of time to explore before the end of the day. Besides, coming here wasn't just about the mystery, and I don't want to let it ruin a fun day with friends."

"The search for balance goes on!" Alice clapped a hand on Annie's shoulder. "On to the next tent!"

The two friends hurried to a tent with a sign that read "Kilt and Caboodle," which featured every accessory one could need for a full-dress kilt.

Annie's eyes widened as she took in the range of merchandise. "Wow, the owner of this business has Mary Beth's flare for packing in tons of stock without it looking like chaos."

"If we don't find a match to your ferrule or sporran here, then matches may not exist!" Alice admitted, impressed by the selection. "Here we go!" She stepped up to a display of pins, cuff links, belt buckles, and brooches. Within seconds, Annie heard Alice muttering in turn as she scanned the display, "Lions ... fish ... knotwork ... stags... swirls. No birds." Alice picked up a pair of cuff links for a closer look. "Here's some thistle, I think. But no juniper."

Annie was perusing a table with a sign bearing the words "Sgian-Dubh." The surface was covered with daggers of different sizes and materials. "Quite a few thistle designs on these ..." she pointed at the sign, "well, whatever that word means. They look like daggers to me."

"It's pronounced 'skeen do,'" a woman said as she stepped through a gap in the tent wall. "It means 'black knife.'"

"We've been admiring the range of your merchandise," said Alice.

The woman's wide smile drew crinkles into the corners of her hazel eyes. "That's what it takes to be a good and true kilt company. Is there any way I can help you?"

Annie showed her the ferrule. "We're looking for information about the design on this ferrule. Do you carry anything like this?"

The woman studied it intensely. After a motionless pause, she answered. "No, I've never carried a design like this one. Our shop carries all the most popular designs." She handed the ferrule back to Annie. "This must be a custom one."

"We suspected as much," said Alice. "Thanks for confirming it for us."

"Always pleased to help." The woman smiled again. "If you are interested in kilt making, by any chance, you won't want to miss Brianna Kincaid's demonstration. She does several sessions throughout the day."

Annie nodded and began to speak when she noticed a sporran hanging on the back wall behind the woman. From her vantage point it looked identical to the one from the attic. "Excuse me, I just noticed that sporran. May I take a closer look?"

Startled, the woman's eyes swung over to the sporran in question. The sealskin was almost identical to Annie's, but it was the clasp design that had caught Annie's attention. "The sealskin? I'm not allowed to sell them in the U.S." She went to the wall and took the sporran off the hook. "The vast majority of sporrans used to be made of sealskin, but the Marine Mammal Protection Act changed that tradition. I like to display it as a nod to the past."

"Is the clasp design juniper?" asked Alice.

The woman chuckled and touched the metal. "You mean the cantle? Yes, it's juniper."

The two friends tried to tamp down their excitement. "I found a sporran with the same design in my grandparents' home." Annie reached into her bag to retrieve a photo and handed it to the woman. "Would it be from the same clan as yours?" she asked calmly.

The woman looked at the photo and then shrugged. "Juniper is the badge for several clans. There's no way of knowing which one of the clans it belonged to."

"Oh." Annie's smile faded a bit. "Well, thank you for

the information. We'll certainly try to make one of the kilt demonstrations."

The woman returned the sporran to its place. "You won't regret it. Enjoy your day."

Annie and Alice stepped out of the tent and walked several yards away before beginning their discussion. They didn't see the woman step to the entrance of the tent, gazing after them. Or how she pulled out a cellphone and made a call, following their progress until they were out of sight.

7

At 10:25 the female contingency from Stony Point met at the MacTavish tent and then wound their way through the crowd to a long, narrow field bordered with spruce, pines, and oak trees, where the falconry event was set to begin any minute. They paused at the edge of the field and scanned the people swarming around its perimeter.

A whistle cut through all the bustle. Annie recognized it as Ian's. She'd heard him use it to call Tartan often enough. Like ladies watching a tennis match, all four heads swiveled over to the left where Ian and Wally were waving at them.

"I'd have something to say to our mayor about being called like a schnauzer," said Alice, "except it does look like he and Wally have staked out a great location for watching the falconry demonstration."

Peggy swung Emily's hand as they all made their way over to the men. "And we can't deny it was effective. I think we could have heard that whistle over at MacTavish's."

Ian wore an apologetic expression as the women came close. "Please forgive my method of communication. The multitudes were pressing in, and we were concerned you wouldn't be able to find us."

"And we wanted to make sure there was enough room for all of us," Wally added. He gestured at the chairs he and Ian had retrieved from the car and had set down right behind the flagged partition.

"We'll make allowances for today," Annie replied as regally as she could while holding back a grin.

Peggy put her hands on her hips. "Yeah. Just don't try it in Stony Point if you ever want a hot cup of coffee at the diner again, Mr. Mayor."

"Ouch!" Ian clapped his right hand over his heart. "That's a hard, hard punishment, don't you think?"

"That's my wife for you, Ian," said Wally. "Hard as nails … when she's not serving folks." His shy grin slid across his face as he looked at the love of his life.

"And being their friend," added Alice.

"And making 'em soup," offered Emily.

"And —" Annie began.

"And that's enough!" Peggy was on the verge of blushing and didn't intend to let that happen. "Didn't we come here to watch the falconers?" She gestured at the field, where a man and woman had strode from opposite ends to meet in the middle and now stood back to back. A huge owl was perched on the woman's well-protected forearm.

Ian maneuvered his way next to Annie and leaned down to whisper, "Did you find out anything?"

"A little," Annie whispered back. "Nothing big. I'll tell you later."

Nodding, Ian turned his attention back to the field, where the two falconers were introducing themselves to the audience.

"Welcome!" The woman spoke first into the microphone that extended from her ear to in front of her mouth. "I am

Master Falconer Brooke, and this is Gandalf, a two-year-old great horned owl. I should point out that falconry today generally refers to hunting with any trained bird of prey." She gestured to the man with her. "Our other Master Falconer, Finley, will assist me in introducing you to the amazing hunting abilities of Gandalf." The dark-haired man with a neatly trimmed beard bowed in response to the audience's applause.

Peggy turned to her friends. "Do you suppose those are their first or last names?"

"Giving their first names makes sense to me, but it's hard to tell," answered Alice.

Wally opened the Games brochure and skimmed through the information. "No names listed for the demonstrators."

"We can ask around afterwards," suggested Ian. Nodding their agreement, the friends turned their attention back to the field. Annie had remained silent, her eyes riveted to the falconers. Were they related in any way to the hawk and rose symbol on the ferrule?

"Gandalf has been with me since I watched him hatch in my kitchen," Brooke told them. "I was the first thing he saw and the first source of his food. He feeds himself now, but he always looks for me when he comes in from the hunt."

As the falconer informed the crowd of Gandalf's ability to carry animals several times his own weight in his powerful talons, the owl stood motionless on the gauntlet that covered her left hand and lower arm. Then she lifted her arm, and the owl extended his wings to glide across the field. The man stepped away from her as she pulled from a pocket a leather lure with a piece of meat attached to the end and began to swing it in circles around her.

"Owls can see moving prey at an astounding rate of speed and hone in on their target." The crowd struggled to keep track of the bird of prey, as it swooped silently closer and closer to the twirling bait. Then it wheeled, picked up speed, and extended its talons to snatch the bait at the end of the leather. Gandalf alighted gracefully on the grass several feet from the falconer to eat its catch.

The audience broke out into cheering and applause. Emily hung onto her father's arm. "Gandalf's wings are *huge*! Could he carry me away?"

Wally looked down at his daughter and grinned into her eyes that were round with amazement. "Nah, you're safe, Em. Sure, he can carry several times his weight like the lady said, but those owls don't weigh more than five or six pounds at the most. Now, if you were only twenty pounds of child, we'd have to guard you real close."

The owl returned to the falconer's gauntlet. "I'll need some help. Are there any children out there who would like to be a part of the next demonstration?"

As children around the perimeter started jumping up and waving for attention, Emily asked her parents, "Can I?"

"Of course," answered Peggy. "Now that Daddy told us you weigh too much for an owl to carry away."

Emily jumped as close to the barrier as she could and waved hard at the male falconer who was walking along the edge selecting the helpers. He paused as he came near the bouncing youngster, waved her to him, and said, "You!"

"Well, now we know what Em will talk about on the first day back at school this fall," said Alice.

"I'm so glad she got picked!" Peggy's eyes followed her

daughter as the falconer, Finley, had the children sit cross-legged in two rows, facing inward.

With the children almost in position, Brooke made another request to the crowd. "I also need four adults to be trees for us, no branches required." In short order four tall adults had taken their places at the end of the two rows of children, on the side opposite from where Brooke and Gandalf stood. Finley took his place behind the "trees" and held out his gloved hand and padded arm.

"Children, each of you is a mouse who does not want to be Gandalf's dinner. An owl can see the tiniest movement, so you must not wiggle, twitch, giggle, or talk. Try to sit so still that you can feel when Gandalf has flown over you." The children glanced at each other and settled into their positions, nervousness on some faces and excitement on others as they became still.

"And 'trees,'" Finley said, addressing the adults next to him, "you also need to stay as motionless as you can. Tree bark can withstand owl talons better than skin and cloth."

Quiet settled over the crowd, each person fixing their eyes on the magnificent bird of prey. At the slightest of signals from his falconer, Gandalf leapt into the air, extending his four-foot wingspan to glide over the heads of the children. Obedient to the falconer's instructions, the children sat as if frozen, the occasional lift of hair as the bird flew over them was the only sign of movement.

It seemed impossible that the large bird could fit between the "trees" as they stood a mere twelve inches apart. But Gandalf rolled back slightly, extended his feet, and landed on Finley's arm in a movement so graceful it could almost be called dainty.

The children, adults, and audience drew in a collective gasp and broke into applause. Emily bounced up onto her knees and hugged herself, giggling with the girl next to her about feeling her hair lift when Gandalf flew over her. The falconers announced a brief intermission and dismissed the helpers. Emily danced across the field to her family and friends.

"That was the coolest thing, ever!" Emily gushed as she ducked under the flag barrier. "Did you see Gandalf poof my hair when he flew by?"

Ian pushed the stop button on his phone's video camera. "Would you like to see it too, Emily?" He made sure the video was back to the beginning and waved the young girl over.

"What a great idea, Ian!" exclaimed Annie. "I was so entranced, I completely forgot about photos or anything."

"So did I," Alice laughed, pulling out her cellphone. "I'll keep it out for the next part of the demonstration."

Emily stood close to the mayor, watching as the great horned owl glided so very close to the top of her head. "I knew he was close, but … wow!"

Peggy leaned close and whispered to Wally, "Am I wrong or is this the first time Em's been speechless since she spoke her first word?"

"Just might be," Wally acknowledged, proud eyes on his daughter.

During the rest of the brief intermission, Ian passed his phone around so everyone could enjoy Emily's experience once more. When the demonstration resumed, this time the main attraction was Athena, a golden eagle. Raised by Finley, the eagle made Gandalf look puny in comparison. The falconer raised his arm, and Athena spread her wings, flying in a circle around the field.

Ian raised his phone to video the giant bird of prey. "Now I really see why the falconers raise their birds from hatchlings. A bird that size could do serious damage."

"It's breathtaking," murmured Annie. "I've seen plenty of bald eagles from a distance, but what a wonder it is to see a golden eagle this close." Her eyes were riveted to the majestic bird and its handler.

"Did you hear what he just said?" asked Wally, amazement on his face. "That bird can dive at speeds up to 150 miles per hour! I've watched my share of fish hawks diving around the Gulf of Maine, but 150 miles per hour?" His mouth puckered, emitting a low whistle.

The friends remained quiet for the rest of the demonstration, fascinated with the fluid efficiency of the raptor whose wingspan dwarfed the tall falconer. As the two falconers bid the crowd farewell, Annie's mind once again turned to the hawk and the rose. Had Brooke or Finley ever seen the design? She tapped Ian on the shoulder.

"Do you think we can catch the falconers before they leave the field?" she asked in a rush. "Maybe they'll know something about the ferrule."

Ian nodded and held out his hand. "Quick! Give it to me." As soon as Annie pulled it out of her bag, he grabbed it and ducked under the barrier. Annie and her friends watched the mayor stride across the field, his steps purposeful.

Alice shared a grin with her friends. "With Ian Butler on your side, who needs a knight in shining armor?"

"Or kilt!" Peggy added. She nudged Annie with an elbow. "Though, I think Mr. Mayor could hold his own in the Bonnie Knees competition."

Annie smiled but didn't reply, too distracted as she tried to surmise what was being said between Ian and Brooke. Her smile faded when the female falconer shook her head after viewing the photo. "It looks like Brooke can't help us."

"Ian better get a move on—Finley is almost off the field," said Wally. "He moves pretty fast for a guy in a skirt."

The friends watched helplessly as Ian thanked Brooke as quickly as he could and followed after Finley and his raptor. Ian hailed the falconer from behind as he tried to catch up to him, but the man appeared to not hear and kept a swift pace until he disappeared into a trailer parked near the field.

After a few minutes, Ian returned across the field. "I'm sorry, Annie. Brooke has never seen the design, although she liked it very much. And Finley—well, I never got to speak to him. He went into a trailer with Athena but didn't respond to my knocking." Although the mayor was well-trained in controlling the emotions in his face from years of local government, his friends knew him well enough to know he was frustrated at not being able to help Annie.

Annie grasped one of Ian's hands and looked him in the eyes. "Ian, you did everything you could. Please don't apologize. Maybe we'll get a chance to speak to Finley later. He probably needed to get Athena into a quiet space after performing for the crowd."

"It wasn't a total loss," Alice declared. "After comparing

you to Finley in his kilt, Peggy thinks you're a shoo-in for the Bonnie Knees competition."

Ian laughed, but didn't move his gaze from Annie's green eyes. "Is that so? Are you ladies going to make me a kilt for next year's Games?"

"That can be arranged," said Peggy. "Girls, we better not miss the kilt-making workshop later."

Ian finally tore his gaze away from Annie, released her hand, and addressed the entire group. "On one condition: No photos of me in a kilt will be allowed to surface during any elections following the Games." He noted the mischievous sparkle in the eyes around him. "Or between them!"

"We promise," Annie sighed, "if we must."

"Where to next?" asked Wally before the women could try to rope him into the competition also.

"We don't want to miss the traditional athletic events like the Caber Toss," Alice declared. "Nothing like watching men and women throwing tree trunks around to reawaken the commitment to physical fitness."

Peggy pulled the Games schedule out of Wally's hand. "And Emily wants to see some dancing."

"Don't forget the sheepdog trials," added Annie.

Alice grinned at Ian. "Or the kilt workshop for us ladies." She leaned over Peggy's shoulder to look at the schedule.

After looking at all the times for the various activities they were interested in, Peggy told them, "If we hurry, we can watch the athletics for awhile before the junior dancing finals start. The sheepdog trials are a bit later."

"Wally and I passed the athletic fields on the way to see the cattle," said Ian. "Ladies, just follow us!"

As the group followed Wally and Ian, walking briskly through the streams of people, Alice slowed Annie for a moment. She whispered, "I bet I know what you're thinking."

With an indulgent look, Annie whispered back, "Give it a whirl."

"Kilt or no kilt," Alice quipped, "Ian Butler is pretty easy to follow."

8

Before Annie could respond to Alice's comment, Peggy turned to wave at them. "Come on, you two! Pick up the slack!"

Emily skipped back to the two friends. "Hurry up, Miss Annie and Miss Alice. You don't want to miss the tree throwing, do you?"

Each woman took one of Emily's hands and caught up to the group. "No, Em, we definitely don't want to miss the tree throwing!"

As they got closer to the athletic fields, the streams of people swelled into a rushing river.

"Oh, I hope there's still a place where we can see what's going on," Peggy chuffed, walking as fast as she could.

Ian scanned the perimeter of the field for any open spaces. He pointed out a corner. "There's an opening at that corner," he said as he lifted his binoculars to check it. "I don't see any 'Keep Off' signs or 'Reserved' notices."

"It's worth a try," said Wally.

"I wonder why it hasn't been taken?" Alice pondered. "It looks like a pretty good position."

"Maybe a large group just left, and others don't have a hawkeyed scout like we do," Annie guessed.

The friends skirted the various gatherings of spectators until they reached the targeted corner, which was still free.

Glancing around, they could see no indication that the area was off limits.

Wally opened a chair and set it down close to the flagged barrier. "Here, Peg—a front row seat." After spreading the quilt for whoever wanted to use it, his wife sat down. Emily first knelt on the blanket but stood up again as soon as the first competition was announced, the Caber Toss.

"Yeah!" Emily exclaimed, barely able to contain her excitement. "It's tree-tossing time!"

A man in a blue-and-green kilt addressed the crowd. "Lassies and lads, welcome to the finals of the Caber Toss competition. In the preliminaries, our competitors endured a grueling elimination to get to this point. Each finalist will be given three attempts, and the best of them will be used to determine the placing. Judges, please take your positions."

Two men, one looking to be in his mid-forties and the other at least a decade older, came from under a tent adjacent to the field. The crowd applauded their arrival.

"Remember, folks," the announcer continued, "the Caber Toss is not judged on the distance of the toss, but on how close to a perfect toss is achieved. I quote from the NASGA rules: 'A perfect toss will pass through the vertical position and land with the small end pointing directly at twelve o'clock, away from the competitor in an imaginary straight line extending from the competitor through the initial landing point and in line with the direction of the run.'" He paused to take an exaggerated gasp of breath. "No sweat."

The audience laughed. "Now I see why they need two judges," Wally commented. "They better be eagle-eyed like Ian."

The kilted competitors who had made it to the final round filed onto the field, queuing up behind a line. Two teenagers, who looked to be no strangers to weight training themselves, bore the caber, a long section of tree trunk tapered at one end to be considerably smaller than the other. Their muscles strained as they stood it on end for the first athlete, tapered side down.

Dressed in royal blue from shirt to kneesocks, the competitor bent from the waist, stabilized the caber against one shoulder and spread his feet wide. Interlacing his hands, he inched them down to the bottom of the caber, as the audience grew quiet in anticipation. In a burst of power, the man hoisted the tree trunk as he stood up straight, stepping backward a few steps as he fought for control. The audience burst into encouraging yells and whistles.

Control gained, the athlete drove his feet into the grass, staggering forward to increase momentum. The back judge trotted after him—his eye fixed on the caber. Then the competitor stopped, and with a grunt heard around the field, he hefted the wood beam into the air and released it.

Applause exploded around the field as the caber landed in a vertical position, paused for a moment, and then crashed to the ground.

"Not bad for a first toss," said Ian. "Looks to be somewhere between one and two o'clock."

Peggy shook her head, amazed. "They do that *three* times? Those Highlanders who came up with the idea of throwing trees must have been an interesting lot."

"No telling what people will come up with when they're bored," Alice quipped.

The judges had finished recording the first throw and signaled for the next competitor, who failed to turn the caber vertical and had to jump aside as it crashed back down near him.

"The first guy made it look rather easy compared to that one," commented Wally. "I wonder how much training he does through the year."

Ian nudged his friend. "Why? Considering a new sport?" He cocked his head to the side as he exaggerated consideration of Wally's build. "I'd have pegged you as more the Haggis Hurl type."

The women laughed at Ian's comments and Wally's reaction, but then they refocused on the competition as the next athlete leaned down to pick up the caber. This man was able to turn the caber, and as it crashed down, they compared its position to that of the first man.

"We don't have the vantage point of the judges, but it looks to me like it's not as good a toss as the first guy," said Alice.

"There's a lot of tossing left," Ian said. "Someone could lead until the very last toss and still come in second."

As if to prove his point, the next athlete not only turned the caber with a deft toss, but its landing position sent the crowd to their feet.

"To beat that toss, someone's going to have to turn it exactly at twelve o'clock!" Wally exclaimed.

Emily pirouetted in excitement and then grabbed her father's arm. "I'm so glad we could come today, Dad!"

Putting his arm around his little dancer, Wally kissed the top of her head. "Me too, Princess. Me too." Father and daughter stood together through the rest of the first round and the following one. The two best tosses from the first round still stood. The Highlander in blue prepared to grab the caber for his third, and last, try.

"I don't see how he can best the leading toss," Alice declared. "Their muscles have to be exhausted by now!"

Peggy reached into her bag to retrieve a tube of sunblock. "Do you suppose these are the same guys who will be doing the Sheaf Toss and Heavy Hammer competitions?" She motioned for Emily to extend her arms for the lotion.

"Some of them," answered Ian. "It's kind of like the Olympics. You have your specialists who sprint or jump or throw the discus, and then you have your decathlon athletes."

Annie nodded, reaching into her bag for a bottle of water. "Nobody can accuse the Scots of being soft."

"That's why there's so many of 'em in Maine," Wally asserted before directing everyone's attention back to the field. "Whoa! Look at that toss!"

The athlete's blue kilt flared as he hefted the end of the caber into the air, his warrior cry echoing across the field. Once again, the spectators jumped to their feet as the caber turned and landed so close to the twelve o'clock position that it seemed impossible. The athlete thrust both arms into the air. The two judges rushed to mark the release and landing spots, and they declared the toss to be the high score thus far.

No matter how the remaining athletes heaved, grunted, or hollered, their tosses could not improve upon the score of the Highlander in blue. After the top three athletes received their laurels, the announcer informed the crowd of the next event: the Haggis Hurl.

The two teenagers toted the caber off the field as volunteers carried a large barrel out and set it upright. Four kilted men trotted a table covered with dozens of what looked to be extremely large sausages from the sidelines and positioned it next to the barrel.

"I've never seen sausages that big before," Peggy said, laughing.

"Nothing can compare to a properly prepared haggis," Alice testified. "It wouldn't be fit for the Highland Games if they made the haggis puny."

Emily looked up at Alice. "Miss Alice, what's the barrel for?"

"The competitors stand on top of it as they throw the haggis," Alice answered. Emily's eyes grew wide at her answer. She added, "Sometimes they use lower platforms for the women or youth challenges." Turning to Ian, she asked him, "It's been several years since I've seen the Games. Do they still do that, Ian?"

"Yes. They did the last time I attended," answered Ian. "Although, when I was here last time, quite a few of the women insisted on using the barrels. Their balance was generally more impressive than the men's, actually."

The announcer took his place at the center of the field again. "Lassies and lads, the rules for the Haggis Hurl are simple compared to that of the Caber Toss. Each competitor will mount the top of the barrel and make his or her best throw. Unless you hit a judge, it will be measured for pure distance. Will the first hurler please take his position?" He started to walk off the field but stopped. "Ah, one more thing. After the official competitors have taken their throws, anyone in the audience wanting to give haggis hurling a try is invited to line up at the north end of the field. Keep an eye on the technique of the successful hurlers." This time, he retreated to the edge of the field near the barrel and table.

Peggy nudged her husband's arm. "Follow the announcer's direction, and maybe you'll be able to test the waters of haggis hurling like Mr. Mayor suggested."

Wally brushed away an overly friendly fly. "I thought he was just teasing," he said. "I dunno. Let me see how they do it first, Peg."

"I think you could do it," his wife insisted. "All those years of casting fishing lines have to work in your favor."

Ian clapped Wally on the shoulder. "She's got a point there, Wally. They have prizes for the best hurls from the audience, you know. Can't hurt to try."

Wally laughed. "A prize. Right. Probably a giant haggis for the family. Let's just watch the competition, all right?" He turned his attention back to the barrel where the first hurler was preparing to scramble on top with a haggis gripped in one hand.

"I think the hardest part would be getting up on that barrel without tipping over," marveled Annie. "It doesn't look like it's the sturdiest of platforms."

The hurler placed his hands on opposite sides of the barrel rim, bent his knees, and sprang up on the barrel, landing like a frog. Annie couldn't resist clapping her hands, a "woo-hoo!" spilling from her lips. Deep concentration was written on the man's face. He straightened until he was standing upright. He drew back his throwing arm and hefted the haggis as hard as he could without tipping himself over.

Ian clapped, his face showing his appreciation of the skill. "Decent first throw. Gives the others a good challenge."

As the rest of the competitors took their turns, it became apparent that the technique of haggis hurling was as varied as its participants. Some techniques appeared to be more successful than others.

"It amazes me that of all those hurlers, only a couple tipped over the barrel," Alice marveled.

"I'd guess a good number of those competitors are fishermen and lobstermen," said Wally. "They learn to balance on anything. They could probably balance on a barrel in an earthquake." He paused for a moment, thinking, and then said, "Maybe I *will* give it a try."

Emily did her best cheerleader imitation. "Go, Dad, go! Go, Dad, go!"

"Save your cheering until it's my turn, Princess," Wally told her. "The women's competition is just starting."

The female hurlers lined up and waited as the two teenagers carried out a wooden platform to set next to the barrel. It was only a few inches shorter than the barrel but wider. At least half of the competitors selected to hurl their haggis from the barrel and made a good show of rising to the challenge.

Annie turned to Ian. "I see what you mean about the women and the barrel. Those lasses were springing up like rodeo queens onto their horses."

"Impressive, for sure," Alice agreed. "Gives new meaning to the phrase 'light on her feet.'"

Ian waved a hand in Wally's direction. "The hurlers from the audience are going to have a hard act to follow."

He stepped behind his friend and started massaging Wally's shoulders like he was a prizefighter preparing to head into the ring. "Better start loosening up."

"All right, all right," Wally muttered, shrugging off Ian's help. "Give a guy some space, Mr. Mayor." But once he had stepped clear of the others, he began to swing his arms in giant circles and squat a few times to warm up his muscles. With a wry grin he asked, "Satisfied? Unless, of course, you'd like to do the hurling yourself?"

"I got myself roped into wearing a kilt next year," Ian reminded his friend. "Don't you think that's enough for one old guy?"

Amidst the laughter that followed, the announcer's voice broke in: "Now it's time for the brave members of the audience to take their chances at the Haggis Hurl."

"Brave or stupid?" Wally added, though he was smiling when he said it. He lightly tugged one of his daughter's pigtails. "When it's my turn at the barrel, cheer with everything you've got, Princess." With a wink at Peggy, he ducked under the fluttering barrier and strode toward the growing line.

Peggy turned to the others, a sheepish look on her face. "Why do I feel like there should be trumpets blasting like he's going out to slay a dragon?"

"Perhaps you read Em too many fairy tales when she was younger," Alice answered, grinning.

"LeeAnn loved *Saint George and the Dragon*," said Annie. "The book was in tatters by the time she moved on to other favorites. I bought a new version with gorgeous illustrations for John and Joanna when they were little."

"Em's favorite books are ballerina and princess ones,"

Peggy reminded her friends. "Now, if there was a book with a dragon princess in a tutu and toe shoes, she'd be all over that story!"

Emily's eyes lit up at her mother's suggestion. "Yeah, yeah! Isn't there a book like that, anywhere?"

"Maybe you could ask at the library?" Since moving to Stony Point, Annie had come to depend on the town's efficient librarians to help her research many of the mysteries that swirled around her. "If there's a story like that, you can be sure Valerie or Grace can find it for you."

Emily tugged on her mother's arm. "Look! Dad's at the barrel. It's time to cheer!" She jumped up and down with her arms in the air. "Go, Dad! Throw, throw, throw!"

"He has to get on the barrel first," Peggy reminded her.

Emily nodded and jumped again. "Jump, Dad! Jump!" The women and Ian clapped along with Emily, their eyes glued to Wally as he gripped a haggis in one hand and prepared to mount the barrel.

"Oh, I hope Wally doesn't break the haggis open when he jumps," Peggy worried. "What a mess that would be! I'd be chewing my nails if Mitzy hadn't worked so hard on my manicure." Peggy's sister, and Stony Point beautician, had decorated her nails with a colorful tartan design for the Highland Games.

His wife needn't have worried. Wally had been springing into boats since he was a youngster, and he easily reached the top of the barrel, haggis intact. Pausing to be sure of his balance, he stood up tall and positioned his feet for the throw. As he took a deep breath, he heard Emily's voice cheering for him.

Rearing his arm back, he hurled the haggis as hard as his workman muscles allowed. The spectators joined his daughter's and friends' cheers as they watched the Scottish delicacy sail through the air and land far beyond the marks of all the previous hurls. The cheers increased when Wally turned toward his family and bowed, his face flushed.

Ian turned to Emily. "Your cheering was very effective! You must come next year if I enter the Bonnie Knees contest."

Em giggled. "OK, Mr. Mayor." She tugged on Peggy's shoulder and beckoned her to bend down so she could whisper, "Mama, how do you cheer for *knees*?"

"We've got a whole year to figure that out, Em," Peggy whispered back.

They turned their attention back to the few remaining haggis hurlers, keeping their eyes trained on the marker indicating Wally's results. When every haggis had been hurled, it was clear he had won the audience round.

The announcer called Wally over to him and said, "I'm hard-pressed to remember a better haggis hurling from an audience member, my lad. What's your name, and where do you hail from?"

Not one to be comfortable speaking to crowds, Wally cleared his throat before he answered, "I'm Wally Carson, and I live in Stony Point." Then he added, "Maine, of course."

"Well, Wally from Stony Point, you might consider signing up for the official competition next year," the announcer suggested. "You've got quite an arm." He opened the sporran hanging from his waist and pulled out a piece of paper. "The Highland Games would like to treat you to a meal at any one of our fine food vendors." He handed the certificate to Wally as the crowd cheered.

As Wally walked back to his family and friends, the announcer called for the athletes of the next competition, the Hammer Throw. The group gathered around Wally, offering their congratulations. He handed Peggy the gift certificate and picked up Emily, twirling her around. "Em, your cheering did the job! I heard you loud and clear."

"Mr. Mayor wants me to cheer for his knees next year," his daughter informed him.

Wally laughed and glanced at Ian. "Good! They're going to need it!"

"Are you going to take the announcer's suggestion and enter the real competition next year?" Alice asked. "Your throw really was impressive."

Wally considered the question for a minute and then shrugged. "Probably not. I'm not thrilled about the idea of jumping onto that barrel in a skirt!"

The first athlete in the hammer-throwing competition, dressed in a black-and-red kilt, stepped into a chalked box and positioned himself with his back to the field, his heels planted near a wood barrier. The announcer reminded the crowd that the feet of competitors were not allowed to move until the throw was completed or the throw would be disqualified. Tuning out the activity around him, the athlete settled the hammer—a 16-pound metal ball attached to a bamboo shaft—on the ground to the right of his body. Bending down, he adjusted his grip on the shaft and then pulled the heavy sphere to the left and into the air. His muscles straining, he swung the weight in a circle three times and released it over his shoulder with a yell.

Ian clapped for the athlete's effort. "Talk about needing strength and balance! I'd forgotten just how impressive the skills of these Highland Games athletes are."

"And this is the 'light' round!" marveled Annie.

The Hammer Throw competition fell into a rhythm of take stance, swing, and release. The 16-pound division was completed and the 22-pound Heavy Hammer competition began. Annie found herself relaxing and putting the mystery of the sporran and ferrule in its proper place. It would be solved in time, and she could enjoy the day and the company of her friends.

An athlete dressed in a kilt of green, navy, and yellow stepped into the box. Someone yelled, "Swing it sound, Hep!" The deep concentration that had been on his face wavered, and he looked around to see from where the shout had come. Then, shaking it off, he bent to his task. Placing the weight to his left, he hefted it and swung. On the third swing the man began to lose balance and was forced to release the hammer early.

Annie had uncapped her water bottle for a sip when Ian realized the hammer was sailing directly at her.

9

"Annie!" Shouting her name, Ian lunged to pull her out of harm's way. As they collapsed on the ground, the 22-pound metal ball and shaft flew over their heads, landing behind them with a dull *thunk*.

Alice, Wally, Peggy, and Emily all dashed to where they lay in a heap. Annie opened her eyes, looking straight into the worried gray eyes of her impromptu bodyguard.

"Are you all right?" he gasped, his arms still clasped around her.

"Yes." Her water bottle had been pressed between Ian and her, and she could feel the dampness spreading to both of them. "Sorry about the water."

"Let her up, you big lug!" Alice ordered Ian, but a smile hovered around her mouth. "Makes no sense to rescue her from a concussion and then squash her ribs."

Ian shook the fog of relief from his mind, let go of Annie, and sprang to his feet. He bent over and offered his hand to help her up. "I hope I didn't hurt you."

Annie shook her head as she straightened her blouse. "Of course you didn't hurt me, Ian. I was distracted, and you saved me from serious harm." She shook her arms and moved her legs. "See? I'm perfectly fine. Thank you!"

The athlete with the wayward throw ducked under the barrier and approached them, his face red with embarrassment.

"I am so sorry! I can't believe I almost hit you! Is there anything I can do?"

Annie couldn't be mad at the repentant young man. "Don't worry … What's your name again?" She couldn't quite remember what the person in the crowd had called him.

"Hep," the man answered, his burly shape still shaking a little. "I've never come so close to hitting anybody before."

Annie reached out to pat Hep on the arm. "Please don't be embarrassed, Hep. It could happen to anyone. As you can see, we're all completely healthy. I'm sure your next two tries will go better."

"I sure hope you're right." Hep glanced back at the Hammer Throw action going on without him. "I better get back now. Thank you for understanding."

The Stony Point group wished him well and watched as he strode back to the line of athletes. "I just can't help liking that man," Peggy declared. "You could tell he really meant what he said."

Annie opened her mouth to reply when her stomach gave a loud rumble everyone could hear.

"Sounds like danger has made you ravenous." Alice nudged her best friend. "Can we pull you away from watching Hep's last throws to get something to eat?"

Annie patted her grumbling stomach and grimaced at the dampness of her blouse. "I think I can be persuaded, as long as they allow wet clothes in the food tents." She pulled her hat back on, retrieving it from the spot where Ian had tackled her.

Peggy dug into her bag. "This is going to sound strange, but I've got a cloth diaper in here." She looked up at the chuckles. "Hey, don't laugh. Diapers will soak up just about anything." Her fingers caught the edge of the cloth and she pulled it out. "Here." She offered it to Annie.

"Thanks, Peggy." Annie gratefully pressed the thick cloth against the damp front of her blouse. "Do you have an extra one? Ian was rewarded for his chivalry with a dousing himself."

Ian waved off the offer. "Don't worry about my shirt. It'll probably be dry before we get to the food area." He looked at Annie as she dabbed away. "Can you walk and wipe at the same time?"

"I think so," answered Annie. "But if I can't, you may want to stay handy, just in case."

Alice leaned close to Peggy and whispered, "I don't think that'll be a problem. Do you?"

"Not at all," Peggy answered with a wink.

Ian helped Wally pick up the chairs, and Peggy folded the quilt and slid it back into her bag. Walking toward the food court, the group stopped to consider what to eat. "Does anyone want anything specific for lunch?" Ian asked, ever the leader.

"I've heard they have some wicked meat pies here," said Wally. "I'd like to see if it's true."

"Are you sure you don't want haggis?" Peggy teased.

Wally slung his arm around his wife's shoulders. "I'm sure, but I'd be glad to buy you one, compliments of the Highland Games."

"As delicious as that sounds, I think I'd like to try a bridie," Peggy countered. "If the puff pastry is made right, it's hard to beat."

Ian pointed out a bright yellow food cart with red lettering proclaiming authentic Scottish food. "That one looks promising." The group gathered around the vendor, reading the menu hanging from the ceiling of the cart.

"What do y'all think about ordering several different dishes, and then everyone can sample them?" asked Annie. "And don't forget the scones!"

Alice gave a thumbs-up for the idea, and there were nods from the others. Emily ended her nod saying, "Mama, what's a bridie?"

"It's a Scottish meat pastry," answered Peggy. "I think you'll like it."

Wally handed Ian the certificate he'd won. "Make sure there are plenty of meat pies to go around." While Ian ordered and their food was being prepared, the others wandered near the different tents to find a good place to settle down for the meal.

"I vote for this tent," Alice gestured at a yellow-stripe tent with the sound of Celtic music coming from inside.

Wally paused, listening to the drums driving a lively tune. "Works for me," he agreed. "I'll go help Ian with the food. Why don't you ladies find us a table?"

The ladies of Stony Point agreed and entered the tent as Wally left them. Picnic tables were packed inside with only a small platform in the front for the musicians. Just as they were reconciling themselves to not being able to fit in the crowded tent, a half-table of people got up to leave.

"Now I know how the town folk feel at the diner," Peggy quipped as she bustled over to the emptied half-table.

"Small triumphs are not to be sneezed at," said Annie, chuckling. "These are good seats for the music too. We can actually see the musicians play."

"I'll wait by the entrance and show the guys where to bring the food," Alice offered. "It's jammed in here!" She wove through the tables filled with people in a festive mood. Reaching the edge of the tent, she stood just outside to watch for Ian and Wally.

While Annie, Peggy, and Emily waited for the others to arrive, the band played a final song and announced that a different band would begin a set in ten minutes. "Oh, I hope the next band is as good as this one," said Peggy. "They had a great sound." She nudged Annie with her elbow. "None of that classic rock stuff."

"Not even U2?" Annie joked back.

"Um, Annie, U2 is from Ireland, not Scotland." Peggy wagged a finger at her friend.

"Oops, good thing Alice wasn't here," Annie responded. "She'd have my hide." Her eyes narrowed. "And how come you knew that when you don't like classic rock, hmmm?"

Peggy dismissed the tease with a wave of her hand. "Some bands—very few mind you—transcend the classic rock label."

The next band filed in through a small gap behind the platform and began to set up. Emily's eyes widened in wonder when she caught sight of the female band member dressed in a gossamer flowing dress of light green and lavender, the golden waves of her hair tumbling down her back.

She whispered to Peggy, "Mom, is she a princess?"

Her mother smiled at her. "I don't know, Em. Maybe you could ask her when the band finishes their set."

As the men of the band positioned a keyboard, two different drums, and several different kinds of wind and string instruments on the platform, Alice came through the main entrance with Wally and Ian behind her. All three sets of arms were laden with food and drinks.

Leading the men through the tables, Alice set two drink carriers in front of Annie and Peggy. "It's a good thing I was watching out for Ian and Wally; the drinks were threatening to slip out of their hands."

"I'm impressed they made it that far." Annie laughed. "Y'all bought enough food to feed William Wallace's entire clan! Is there anything left in the food cart for everyone else?"

"I'm sure there's still plenty of haggis left," Wally said as he placed a stack of boxed meat pies and bridies next to the drinks.

"We need to toast Wally's hurling abilities," said Ian. "The vendor wouldn't hear of taking any extra money after seeing the certificate. It covered our entire lunch." He handed a box of scones to Annie to pass around the group.

Peggy cocked an eyebrow as she pulled two cups of soda out of the carrier, setting one in front of Emily. "These folks sure take their haggis hurling seriously!"

"And that is a good thing," Annie added as she reached over for a drink. "This is a fine feast. The food smells delicious." Her eyes roamed over the different boxes of food. "I can't decide what to try first."

Alice grinned, standing to bend over the boxes and transfer a bridie and a meat pie to her paper plate with a fork. "Then let your bossy friend decide for you." She briskly cut each pastry in two and transferred a half to Annie's plate. "That'll get you started."

"If you have any appetite left when you've eaten those,

try the beef sausage rolls," Ian suggested after politely wiping his having just taken a bite of one of the juicy sausage rolls. "This is really good."

Annie stared down at her suddenly laden plate. "LeeAnn will be most appreciative of my friends' efforts to make sure I don't waste away from starvation. Now you will have to help me work off all these calories!" She selected the half-moon–shaped meat pie and took a bite. "Mmmmm."

The volume of chatter inside the tent lowered as the female singer introduced the first song. "We can think of no better way to begin our music than with *Ca' the Yowes*, a song written by Scotland's own Robert Burns." Behind her, a member of the band raised a flute and began a soft melody. "For those who are not familiar with the song, 'yowes' are ewes, female sheep."

A fiddle and keyboard were added, and the audience seemed to pause from eating and talking, anticipating the entrance of the singer's voice. It came, pure and delicate yet also strong. The song called to mind hills blanketed with heather and abiding love.

Wally swallowed a bite of meat pie. "Not exactly my kind of music," he observed, "but the singer has a good set of pipes on her."

"I think she's beautiful," Emily sighed. "I wonder if she likes to dance too." The girl found it hard to comprehend anyone not loving to dance as much as she. Not able to pull her eyes away from the golden-haired woman, Emily nibbled on a scone.

The band began the second song, *Wild Mountain*

Thyme, the singer's eyes slowly roaming over the audience from the back to the closer tables.

Annie rested her cheek in her right hand, caught up in the gentle lilting strains of the music and voice. "I wonder what it's like to be given a voice like hers. How many hours has she practiced over the years to develop her gift?"

"Looks like singing isn't the only thing she's been practicing," Alice muttered under her breath, when the woman began the next song.

Annie turned to look at her friend sitting beside her. "What do you mean?"

"Can't you tell who she's singing to? You know, flirting?" Alice jerked her gaze toward Ian.

Annie shook herself out of the near trance the music had put her in and looked between the singer and the man at her left side. Sure enough, Alice's observation was sound. While the woman's gaze had previously been roving from person to person, she was now singing directly to Stony Point's mayor:

"I will build my love a bower,
By yon clear crystal fountain,
And on it I will pile,
All the flowers of the mountain.
Will you go, lassie, go?"

The song went on, but the eyes of the singer did not. Alice and Annie stole glances at Ian, expecting to see some reaction from him. But the man was deep in conversation with Wally and was not looking toward the platform.

Annie leaned to whisper in Alice's ear, "Surely she'll realize he's not noticing and find some other man to serenade."

"Was that just a hint of jealousy speaking?" Alice whispered back.

Annie didn't answer. She didn't have to. Alice gave her a look of understanding and handed her a pack of Scottish shortbread. Giving her friend a wan smile, Annie broke open the shortbread and took a nibble of the buttery sweet.

Toward the end of the song, Ian and Wally concluded their discussion, and Ian returned his attention to the performers. The singer's smile widened, and her blue eyes wooed the unsuspecting man as she sang:

"If my true love she'll not come,
Then I'll surely find another,
To pull wild mountain thyme,
All around the purple heather.
Will you go, lassie, go?"

The face of the man who had spent years in military and political service grew as still as a marble bust. Then he turned his attention away from the musicians once more and focused on Annie, asking her if she was enjoying the shortbread. Annie smiled and offered him a piece. Until the end of the song, the two kept their eyes on each other, as though the singer did not exist.

But Alice and Peggy, intrigued by the boldness of the woman, felt no need to ignore her. They enjoyed the rest of their lunch while keeping track of the performance and the woman's gaze, which moved over to Annie after a while.

Then, the singer announced the final song, *The Banks o' Doon*. About halfway through the lyrics her eyes returned to Annie. Peggy leaned over the table toward Annie and Ian. Positioning her arm as though to brace herself but actually trying to shield her mouth from the musicians, she whispered, "Um, Annie, you might want to take a look and listen to the singer."

Both Ian and Annie reluctantly turned their focus from each other to the performance. As soon as she saw Annie's attention had been won, the woman looked straight into her green eyes and sang:

"With lightsome heart I put a rose,
Full sweet upon its thorny tree;
And my false lover stole my rose,
But, ah! He left the thorns wi' me."

When she began the final verse, her eyes turned away from Annie to finally perform for the entire audience.

"What was that all about?" Peggy mouthed to her friends.

Bafflement covered Annie's features. "Your guess is as good as mine. I'm going to see if I can talk to her as soon as the music stops."

"I think Wally and I should accompany you," said Ian. Wally nodded his agreement.

Annie paused, and then reluctantly agreed. "Just be sure you don't intimidate her. I really want to be able to find out what she meant by singing that verse specifically to me. A false lover? Stealing her rose? What's that got to do with me?" She turned to Ian. "Or you for that matter? Why she was flirting with you long before she noticed me?"

"It's been a long time since I've been that startled or uncomfortable," Ian admitted. "Look, they're ending. Let's go."

The band was taking their bows to the enthusiastic applause of the audience. Had the two members of the Stony Point group not been singled out for such unusual attention, they would also have been vigorously clapping. Instead, Annie and her two bodyguards stood to move toward the platform, while Alice, Peggy, and Emily tidied the table, although their eyes followed their three friends.

As they approached the area where the musicians were gathering their instruments, Annie raised her voice above the noisy crowd. “Excuse me, Miss! May I talk to you for a moment?”

The sapphire eyes of the beautiful woman barely brushed Annie’s face before she turned toward the back of the tent. When Annie and the men began to follow her, two burly men in kilts who had been stationed by the exit stepped forward to block their path.

“I only want to ask her about the last song she sang,” Annie explained.

The two men crossed their arms, remaining silent.

Ian took her hand, lightly squeezing, “It’s OK. Let’s get back to the others.”

Annie, though disappointed, nodded to the kilted men and allowed Ian to draw her away, with Wally following them. As soon as they were a safe distance from them, Ian said to the other two. “Quick! Maybe we can go out the front and still catch her behind the tent.”

The three hurried, trying to make as little commotion as possible, to the table where they had eaten. Alerting Alice and Peggy quickly, they all rushed for the entrance.

10

Fairly tumbling out into the sunshine, the two men, three women and one little girl blinked as their eyes adjusted to the brightness.

"This way!" Ian waved for the group to follow him around the right side of the large tent toward the exit where the singer had fled. Wally scooped Emily up into his arms so she wouldn't be trampled.

Before the friends reached their destination, a large shadow passed over them. Alice glanced up and shrieked, "Everybody, duck!" Pulling Peggy, who was next to her, down with her, she huddled against the side of the tent as the huge golden eagle from the demonstration swooped over their heads, talons extended forward. Wally turned with his back toward the raptor, hunching over to provide as much protection for his daughter as possible. Ian threw his arm around Annie and crouched, seeking to do the same.

The bird's shadow left, and the group started to rise from their defensive positions until Emily pointed over her father's shoulder. "Daddy! She's coming back!" As one entity, the six bewildered people sank again into a tight knot, sheltering against the tent canvas.

Two more times the golden eagle harried them, descending close enough to have been able to harm before pulling up just inches from their heads. At last Athena did not turn back on them, but soared over the tent tops and away.

After staying crouched under Ian's arms for a few minutes, Annie drew in a shuddering breath. "Do you think it will come back?"

"Mercy, I hope not!" Alice exclaimed. "This is more excitement than I bargained for on my semi-vacation." Her eyes scanned the sky for any signs of the raptor.

Ian had remained stalwart during the attack, and his voice reflected a calm the others did not share. "Athena could have attacked at any time instead of simply passing over us. I don't think she will harm us, even if she does come back."

"Well, let's not make it easy for her, if she does," inserted Wally. "I say it's time to move on to somewhere else."

Peggy nodded her agreement with her husband's suggestion. "The singer is surely long gone by now, so why don't we go watch some dancing." She glanced at her daughter still clasped in Wally's arms. "How does that sound, Em?"

Emily's eyes darted around them. "OK—as long as Athena doesn't follow us."

Wally's arms tightened around her. "I won't let her near you, Princess."

"There's something else I think we need to consider," said Ian. "But let's find a tent in which to talk for just a minute before we head to the dance venue." The sound of a different band could be heard in the tent where they had eaten lunch, so the mayor looked around at the other nearby tents. "The one over there sounds pretty quiet."

The others followed him into the tent and gathered around an empty table. "What's on your mind?" Alice asked once they were settled.

Ian looked at Annie apologetically. "With the events of the last hour or so, I'm beginning to suspect you have stumbled onto a secret that is potentially dangerous. I'm concerned for your safety, Annie."

"Do you think Hep threw the hammer at Annie on purpose?" asked Peggy.

Ian considered her question for a moment. "I don't know. He certainly seemed sincere when he apologized, but I admit I'm rather stunned by everything that's happened."

"He seemed awfully embarrassed," said Annie. "I really don't see how he could have faked it so well."

"But then again, we didn't stick around to see his other throws," pondered Alice.

Annie admitted, "That's true. And even if Hep's throw was truly unintentional, there's no way the singer's actions—or the eagle's for that matter—were random."

"That's obvious to all of us," said Wally. "Annie, you sure do have a way about you for finding mischief!"

Annie sat up straight, a wry grin spreading across her face. "I don't find the mischief, Wally. It finds me!"

"Be that as it may, I think we need to consider whether it might not be safer for you if we leave," Ian gently suggested. "You can still research the sporran and ferrule, just at a distance from the people who seem to be shaken up by your presence."

Annie dug into her bag, pulling out her notebook and pen. "And who are those people?" She flipped open the notebook and began scribbling names. "Apparently, the falconer, Finley. But we never even talked to him."

"Maybe Brooke told him about Ian's questions," suggested Peggy.

"Maybe," Annie agreed. Annie wrote "singer" below "Finley—falconer." "I wish the falconers had given their full names," she said, "and I don't remember the name of the singer. Does anyone?"

The adults looked at each other, shaking their heads. "I don't think they ever introduced themselves," said Alice. "Or maybe I was too distracted by all the food when they first started."

"Now that you mention it, I'm certain the individual band members were never introduced," said Ian. "The band name was … " His voice trailed off.

Peggy drummed her manicured nails on the table before remembering. "Celtic Mist!"

"Yes!" Annie jotted down the band name. "Now we just need to find out the name of the lead singer."

Ian cleared his throat, drawing the others' attention. "We've strayed from our original discussion. The question before us is whether we should leave the Games and take you safely home to Grey Gables."

Annie sat quiet for a moment before answering. "I see no reason to leave and force everyone else to miss out on hours more of fun. Ian—you said yourself that if Athena had been sent to harm, she would have.

So, obviously she wasn't. And the singer also did no harm. Music doesn't maim." She tried to lighten things with a small laugh. "We haven't seen the dancing for Emily or the sheepdog trials, which I know you want to see."

"And don't forget the kilt-making demonstration," added Alice. "We might meet some other crafters from other Maine towns. I know Mary Beth would appreciate that."

Ian pulled a white handkerchief out of his pocket and waved it. "I surrender. I know when I'm beat."

Wally clapped him on the shoulder. "You gave it a good try, Ian. But it's impossible to change the mind of stubborn womenfolk. It's like trying to dictate Maine weather."

"Does that mean we can stop talking and go watch the dancing now?" asked Emily.

The defeated man tucked his flag of surrender back into his pocket and smiled at her. "Yes, Em. That's exactly what it means."

The dancer sprang out of her chair and tugged on Wally's arm. "Come on, Dad. Mr. Mayor says we can go! I don't want to miss it!"

"Hold on a sec," Wally told his daughter and quickly consulted the Games schedule and map before standing up and taking her hand. "Now I know where we need to go. You wouldn't want to end up watching the Highland cattle dancing, now would you?"

Emily giggled and rolled her eyes. "Cows can't dance!" The mood lightened, and the adults put aside the baffling events that had preceded and followed the dancing girl out of the tent and toward Stage 3. Ian, however casual his demeanor, kept his eyes moving from crowd to sky, ever vigilant.

The group from Stony Point spied some seats located in the center of the rows from where they would be able to see every part of the stage, including the pipers standing on the edge of the platform. As they arranged themselves, Emily sitting on her father's lap for an even better vantage point, the next Premier dance category was announced: the *Seann Triubhas*.

Three girls who looked to be in the twelve- to fourteen-year age range stepped onto the platform and formed a line, leaving about five feet of space between them. With their hands on their hips and their heels together with their toes turned out, they stood like statues as the piping began. Then, hinging at the waist, they solemnly bowed and began their dance, stepping to the side and back before moving in a circle on one foot at a time—first the right and then the left.

Emily leaned forward in her father's lap, as though to be as close to the movement as possible, her eyes darting back and forth between the three dancers before settling on one. "The dancer in red is the best," she whispered to Peggy who was sitting next to her. The girl in the red tartan sprang more quickly and lightly, keeping perfect time to the music. Further into the song, one of the other dancers mistakenly turned in the opposite direction from the other two. The young dancer from Stony Point sighed in understanding. The first time Emily had danced in a recital she realized that performing in front of a bunch of people you don't know was harder than she had expected. But she was getting used to it now. She felt sorry for the girl who was several years older than her and yet still showed such nervousness.

After two and a half minutes of dancing, the song ended with a final bow, and the three dancers trotted off the stage to make room for the next group. By the time the next four groups had taken their final bows, the folks from Stony Point had developed a strong appreciation for the difficulty of the *Seann Triubhas* dance.

Alice leaned over toward Peggy and Annie, "You always hear about the Highland Fling, but this one looks more difficult to me." She paused to read the brochure to see what would be the next dance in the competition. "Oh—the Sword Dance is after this. That's a cool one too."

Emily tore her gaze from the dancers approaching the platform. "Miss Alice, have you ever danced the Sword Dance?"

"Oh, no, Emily," Alice answered with a laugh. "That's too complicated for me! But I bet *you* could master just about any dance you want to."

Peggy had not missed her daughter's rapt expression while watching the *Seann Triubhas*. "Something tells me it's a good thing we're going to that kilt-making demonstration." She moved her eyes to the feet of the dancers lining up for the dance. "And I better start saving for new dance shoes. Em doesn't have any like those. I'll have to ask around about them."

Emily turned to her with eyes sparkling with

excitement. "Really, Mom? Can I learn Highland dancing too? Maybe even dance at the Highland Games?"

"If it's what you want to learn, Em," Peggy answered. "I figure now's the time to try different things and see what you want to do the most. How can you know if you don't try lots of dances?"

Emily whispered, "Thank you, Mom!" and turned her eyes back to the three dancers on the platform, who had already bowed and were beginning their steps in a circle. Immediately, a girl in a sky-blue kilt stood out to all who watched. Her jumps were lighter, higher, more precise and full of joy. To Emily, it was as though only one girl were dancing, and she did not take her eyes off the dancer until she had bowed and disappeared off the platform. Emily leaned back against her father and murmured, "Beautiful!"

All the *Seann Triubhas* competitors had danced and awaited their scores. To no one's surprise, the dancer in the sky-blue kilt was declared the winner. Her name was Kyla Bell. The groups for the Sword Dance were called, and the audience took the chance to talk among themselves.

"So, what do you think of the dancing, Mr. Mayor?" Peggy asked Ian.

Ian had divided his time between enjoying the performances and observing the audience and the activity in the vicinity. "I'm impressed by the mastery shown at such a young age," he answered. "Some of the other dancers looked much older than the first-place winner. This has sparked an idea I'm going to research once I get back to the office."

"Is it top secret or can some of your constituents be in on this idea too?" asked Alice.

Ian grinned. "Actually, getting some opinions might not be a bad idea. What do you think of having a Robert Burns Day in Stony Point? After all, most of the town's original settlers were from Scotland. I was thinking about having a Highland dance group come."

"I love the idea, Ian!" Annie exclaimed.

"So do I," added Alice. "Just don't force us to eat haggis."

"I'm not sure you can have a Robert Burns Day without haggis," Wally teased.

Alice leaned over and playfully whacked Wally on the head with her brochure. "I didn't say Ian couldn't have it ... he just can't force us to eat it. There's probably someone in town crazy enough to want to try it."

"I think it's a great idea, haggis or no haggis," said Peggy. "But give me plenty of warning so I can haggle some time off with the boss. I might even be able to convince Marie to bake up some scones for the event."

"There's a good deal of research to do, and I'll have to run it past the town board," Ian said. "But I'll keep you posted, Peggy, and if it's approved, I'd certainly appreciate your help." He looked around at his other friends. "And everyone else's."

"You'll have it, of course," Annie assured him. "Pitching in is one of the things the people of Stony Point do best." When Annie had first come to Stony Point she had wondered if she'd ever feel comfortable there, New England being so different from the South. But it wasn't long before she learned to appreciate those differences; she also saw the many ways in which the people were the same, at heart. And for Annie, the heart was what mattered the most.

Emily tugged on her father's shirt collar and whispered to him, "Dad, can we stop talking? The Sword Dance is starting. See the swords they put on the stage?"

Wally looked at the stage and saw that his little princess was right. "OK, Em. I'll be quiet during the dancing ... just for you." The other adults hid their smiles and tucked their conversation in their pockets to pull out later.

Three dancers had positioned themselves behind three sets of crossed swords. As with the *Seann Truibhas*, the piping played for half a minute before the girls bowed and began their dance. They started on their toes behind the swords before winding their way between the swords with leaps and intricate steps. Although sounds coming from the crowds milling around the platform were constant and at times loud, the audience tuned it all out as they watched the breathtaking dance.

When the three girls had bowed and were leaving the platform, Wally dared to ask Emily a question. "Which do you like best, the Sword Dance or the first one?"

His daughter pursed her lips as she thought about the two dances, and then shrugged. "I like them both. The swords are cool, but the steps in the first one looked fun too." Her eyes grew starry. "Especially when Kyla Bell danced. I hope I can dance as beautifully as her when I'm her age!" Only the arrival of another trio of dancers drew her out of her reverie.

As they watched trio after trio, the adults from Stony Point spent as much time watching Emily as they did the dancers. Her happiness was contagious. Once the winner of the Sword Dance competition was announced, the group rose to leave. They didn't want to miss the finals of the sheepdog trials.

Emily walked between her parents, still gushing about Kyla Bell.

Watching ahead of them to make sure they weren't steered off course by the crowds, Ian noticed Emily's new idol just ahead of them. "Em, Kyla's right up there." He pointed her out. "Why don't you go talk to her?"

Emily followed the mayor's signal and hope sprang into her eyes. Once again Peggy dug the Highland Games brochure out of her bag. "Here, Em. Maybe she'll autograph it for you." She handed it to her with a pen. The little family quickened their pace to catch up with the lithe dancer.

When they got close, Wally called for the girl's attention. "Excuse me, Miss Bell."

Kyla was still wearing her sky-blue kilt, but had changed into a pair of canvas shoes. Her black dance shoes hung around her neck, the shoelaces tied together. Her light brown hair was still pinned up in the style she had worn for the competition. Kyla's head turned as she looked for who had addressed her. Wally nudged his daughter's arm and whispered, "Go ahead, Em!"

The floodgates opened. "I loved your dancing! I've

never seen anyone dance like that. How did you learn all those steps and leaps? How many years have you been dancing?" Emily took a deep breath as if to fuel many more words but suddenly stopped, as if overwhelmed.

The object of the gushing broke into a wide smile. "Oh, thank you! What's your name?"

"Emily."

Kyla held out her hand. Instead of shaking it, Emily placed the brochure and pen in it. "Would you give me your autograph?"

"Oh, I'd love to," Kyla replied, opening the pen. "I've been dancing since I was five, and I learned the Seann Truibhas by practicing it over and over and over until I was dancing it in my sleep. I still need lots more years of work to perfect it, but I worked hard enough to make Premier level before I turned ten."

"I started when I was five too!" Emily exclaimed.

Kyla wrote on the brochure: "To Emily, my sister in dance. Kyla Bell." She handed the pen and brochure back to her. "I hope I'll get to watch you dance here soon, Emily. I have to run now; my uncle and his dogs are in the sheepdog finals. I don't want to miss their run."

"We're going there too!" Emily told her.

Kyla smiled at the group gathered around. "I'd love to sit with Emily during the finals. May I join you?"

Emily and Kyla looked toward Peggy and Wally, waiting for their response.

"We'd be glad to have you with us, Kyla," said Peggy. With a wink toward Annie she added, "Maybe you can help us find a good, safe place to watch from."

"Oh! I know a couple of places where the view is just right," said Kyla.

As the group from Stony Point followed Kyla through the press of people, Emily's face was brighter than the summer day.

11

As the group approached the large field, which was cordoned off with portable orange fencing for the sheep dog trials, Kyla steered them to a knoll located behind the mid-field point. "This is where I like to watch. From here, you can see all the obstacles." She pointed to an opening in the barrier to their left, a pen of sheep filling its gap. "They'll start over there where they release the sheep, and then the dogs have to drive the sheep through each of the gates and posts. They get a point for each sheep that goes through each obstacle."

Kyla moved her hand over toward the right. "When all the sheep are herded into the pen over there, and the gate is closed by the dog's master, the time will be marked. If it's more than twelve minutes, the team is disqualified. That's called 'timing out.'"

"Do many teams time out?" asked Ian. The competition field was on the other side of the fairgrounds from the falconers' trailer, but his eyes still moved from field to sky sporadically.

"It happens more often in the single-dog category," answered Kyla. "Sheepherding is a lot more tricky with just one dog. It doesn't take much to scatter sheep, but that's what makes it fun to watch. You never know what they might do!"

Peggy straightened her quilt out on the grass. "What category is your uncle in?"

Kyla smiled. "He's in the single-dog group. He used to do both single- and two-dog, but he says he likes the challenge of single-dog best. His dog is the smartest border collie ever." She looked over at her new friend. "Wait until you see him, Emily."

Peggy finished preparing the quilt, and Emily flopped down on it, patting the space next to her. "Here, Kyla, sit with us!" Once her new friend sat, taking the dance shoes she had tied together to hang around her neck and placing them beside her, Emily asked, "Do you know why they're called border collies?"

Kyla smoothed the fabric of her kilt over her knees. "When you have family with a sheep farm and dogs, get to know border collies pretty well—but there are a lot of ideas about where the name 'collie' came from. One thing I do know—because my uncle told me—the sheep industry of the areas near the border between Scotland and England grew and grew. So about a hundred years ago, they gave the collies that made it possible their own name—border collies."

"Now that's something I didn't know," said Alice. "Em—I used to wonder about that too. I thought at first it might have something to do with their markings, but then I realized they didn't make a border. I never took the time to find out the real story." Movement at the end of the field where the starting gate was located caught her attention. "Oh, are they starting?"

A kilted announcer walked far enough onto the field

for the crowd to see him. "Lassies and lads, the first final of the Sheepdog Trials will be Single-Dog Herding. Using just their voice and staff, the shepherds must direct their dog to move five sheep through the gates to the pen on the far side. Our judge for the day is Scottie Shaw. Will the first competitor please take your place!" The announcer retreated, and the judge strode onto the field.

Annie chuckled when she saw the man's clothing. "I'm guessing Scottie won't be participating in the Bonnie Knees competition." Though the man was wearing a kilt, he was wearing it over a pair of khaki pants. He also wore a wide, brimmed hat.

Wally harrumphed. "That's the only way *I'd* wear a kilt too."

"Maybe the judge is sensitive to the sun," Ian suggested. "A fair amount of people are having to watch out for sun exposure these days, either because of medication they're taking, skin cancer, or just because their skin burns easily."

Annie sobered. "I hadn't thought of that, Ian. You have a very good point."

Kyla shyly entered the discussion among the adults. "Mr. Shaw has judged at the Games since before I was born. He started wearing pants with his kilt when I was just starting to dance. Mom said he had a knee replaced and has been wearing the pants ever since. She used to tease him about being vain, but it made him turn red, so she stopped."

"Red in embarrassment or anger?" Peggy's question came out in a rush, as though she couldn't resist the question.

Kyla half-smiled. "Maybe both? But I like Mr. Shaw. He always asks about my dancing and comes to watch when he can. Today, our competitions were too close together for him to come." She kept her eyes on the area where the shepherds positioned themselves at the start of each run. "Watch him while the sheep are out. He's a great judge and knows everything about sheep and training dogs."

As the first shepherd, a woman in jeans and light denim jacket with rolled-up sleeves, took her place, Annie watched the judge. Had he known her grandfather? Shaw was not one of the clans that used the juniper for its badge. Was he perhaps related to one of the families that did? If he'd been judging at the Games for so many years, maybe he would know something about the sporran or ferrules. Should she try to talk to him after the finals? Glancing at Ian and thinking of the concerns he had voiced, Annie was no longer as eager to share the photos of the items, as she had been when they first arrived at the Games. Something told her to wait and watch.

There was plenty to watch. The woman held a staff in one hand, and a whistle was in her mouth. Her border collie stood beside her, alert and waiting for her first command. Once the volunteers released the black-faced sheep, the shepherd sounded two short whistles. Instantly, the dog moved toward the sheep. As he neared the sheep, another whistle came—*wheet-weeeo*. In response, the dog began to move clockwise around the sheep until he was behind his charges, and the sheep began to move toward the first obstacle.

When the sheep approached the targeted gate, there came another whistle command: *hee-hee-hee-hee.* The collie immediately slowed down to prevent the sheep from missing the gate.

Ian released a low whistle himself. "Wow! That is one well-trained dog!"

Kyla turned toward the mayor. "Mrs. Grant's been training dogs for a long time. She breeds border collies, and she can read a pup like a book. Uncle Leathan always says she's his stiffest competition."

One of the sheep broke free from the others and started back toward the holding pen. *Who-hee-who* sounded from Mrs. Grant's whistle.

"That whistle signals Haggis to turn around and bring the stray sheep back to the group," Kyla informed the others.

A short laugh escaped Alice's mouth. "Haggis is his name? Poor doggie!" She paused, watching as the dog wheeled around to gather the wandering sheep. "Doesn't seem to bother him, though. Look at how he's fast but smooth, so the sheep don't startle."

Ian was staring at Haggis in sheer admiration. "I wonder if I should get a border collie to keep Tartan in line."

"Is Tartan a sheep?" asked Kyla, no longer shy. One slender hand felt around her bun of hair while she talked, checking the pins and making adjustments where needed.

Emily giggled. "Tartan is Mr. Mayor's dog." She leaned close to her new friend and whispered. "Sometimes Tartan doesn't listen when they're on the beach, and he runs off over the rocks or chases the birds. And one time Tartan got his leash loose and walked right into The Cup & Saucer when Mr. Mayor was eating lunch!"

Kyla covered her mouth and tried to hold in a laugh.

"It's all right, Kyla," said Ian. "Everyone in the diner laughed, and there's no reason you shouldn't too." A rueful grin spread across his face. "I could definitely use some pointers from Mrs. Grant or your uncle. Tartan's a great dog, but his obedience is spotty, at best."

"What breed is Tartan?" the young girl asked.

"He's a standard schnauzer," answered Ian, "and quite a character. I try to make sure he gets enough exercise and social time, but sometimes my job does get in the way. That's when he tends to get mischievous."

A burst of applause and cheers brought the group's attention back to the field, where Haggis was herding the last of the five sheep through the final gate and into the pen.

"That was quick!" Kyla gasped. "Uncle and Clyth are really going to have to move it to beat them!" Her eyes moved to the opposite side of the field to try and see the identity of the next competitor. When a man with a dark green kilt and short, precisely trimmed blond hair approached the starting post, she relaxed. "That's not Uncle Leath. I think he's new. I don't recognize him or his dog."

It was clear from the first whistled command that both shepherd and border collie were not as accustomed to the timed competition. Compared to Mrs. Grant, the whistles were more tentative, and the dog's response less precise, which led to much good-natured laughter from the audience as sheep darted this way and that.

Annie covered her eyes for a minute. "I don't know if I can bear to watch. I feel so sorry for the shepherd!"

Ian placed a hand on her shoulder. "He's just getting the bad run out of his system. People usually learn more from their mistakes than from their shining moments." He paused, thinking. "When you first started crocheting—and each time since then when you try a new technique—don't you gain more from those messy first tries?"

Annie widened her hands enough to peak at Ian. "Well, yes. But I didn't have to parade those messy starts in front of hundreds of people." She winced at the thought.

"Fair enough," admitted Ian. He gave a quick laugh. "Here's another example, one Alice might even remember." He turned to their auburn-haired friend. "Do you recall my first speech when I ran for mayor the first time?"

Alice's mouth pursed, and she blew out a long breath. "Do I!" She turned to Annie. "You think this is painful? It's nothing compared to Ian's crash and burn. He had us all so confused."

"She's not exaggerating," Ian ruefully admitted. "I was so nervous I mixed up my note cards right before the speech. To this day I don't actually know what I said, and I'm OK with that. Nothing I experienced in the Navy prepared me for campaign speeches." He slowly shook his head, lost in the embarrassing memory. "But I never made the same mistake again. And I learned how to be a clear public speaker."

Annie's hands dropped away from her face. "Although I'm having a hard time picturing you in that state, I'll take your word on it. You're an excellent speaker now." She dared to take a look at what was happening on the field. "I just realized ... they made it into the finals, so they actually did very well for their first year, didn't they?"

"That's right!" Kyla's face brightened. "Their first run must have been much better than this one. Newbies almost never make the finals. I wonder if something happened in between the runs to throw the dog off."

Annie glanced around at her friends. "I'd imagine there's all sorts of things that can happen at such a large event as this." She smiled into Ian's eyes. "Thank you, Ian, for sharing your story. It has given me a whole new perspective."

Ian bowed slightly, and he made an attempt at a Southern drawl. "My pleasure, Ma'am."

Alice winced. "Oh, Ian. Don't try a drawl again until Annie's given you some private lessons."

The clapping of the audience eclipsed the laughter of the group, as the green-kilted shepherd shut the gate of the pen behind the last sheep. Wiping his face with a melodramatic flourish, he bowed to the crowd and received an appreciative response. The Stony Point folks and their young friend clapped and whistled enthusiastically.

"In a few years, your uncle might have another challenger to watch out for," Peggy said as she clapped.

Kyla bobbed her head in agreement. "Uncle Leath likes competition. He says it benefits the breed too." She turned her head to see which shepherd was coming next and bounced up onto her knees. "My uncle is next!"

She and Emily jumped up and pressed close to the barrier. "Come on, Clyth! Move those sheep!" Kyla yelled.

The broad-shouldered man now standing by the starting post looked over toward the group and tipped his hat in acknowledgement. "Clyth is Uncle Leath's collie," Kyla explained.

Emily kept jumping as the sheep were released and the shepherding began. The rest of the group silently watched the movement of dog and sheep. By now they understood the meaning of most of the whistles they heard. *Wheet-wheeo-wheet-wheet* for "move away from the sheep" and *whee-who* for "go counterclockwise around the sheep," although Leath used the common short vocal commands of "Get out!" and "Way to me!"

At one point two sheep began to stray from the others, but Clyth responded to Leath's "Look back!" and *who-hee-who* with such speed they only had time to move a couple steps away before being herded into the small flock and onward to the next gate.

"It's going to be close," Kyla said as the sheep neared the pen.

Clyth moved the sheep through the final gate and into the pen, lowering himself to the ground at his owner's *hee-hee-hee-hee* and "That'll do!" The man confidently swung the pen gate shut, and the crowd jumped to its feet, whistling and applauding.

As the judge was conferring with the timekeeper, Annie gazed at Kyla's uncle. Noticing he wore a sporran, she looked around until she located an older gentleman with a sporting scope. Her friends watched as she slipped through the spectators to where the man stood. In short order, all the Stony Point adults saw her speak to him and then lean over to peer into the scope. When she straightened again, she shook the man's hand in thanks and hurried back to the group. Glancing over at Kyla to make sure she and Emily were occupied, she whispered her find first to Ian and then her other friends. Kyla's Uncle Leath was wearing a sporran with a cantle extremely similar, if not identical, to the one Annie had found in her attic.

After several more runs, the announcer and Scottie Shaw moved to the center of the field to declare the winner. "This year's final was a heart-stopper," the announcer began. "Scottie agrees this year's competition is indicative of how strong border collie breeding and training is in New England." The crowd applauded but showed its impatience.

"But enough gabbing," the man continued on cue. "Our second fastest time was achieved by Patrice Grant." He paused as the crowd reacted with cheering. "And our winner, for the second year in a row, is Leathan Gunn."

Kyla threw her hands over her head in triumph and danced a happy quick step, Emily trying her best to follow her. Leathan strode out to the center to accept the prize and to shake hands with the judge, Clyth obediently at his side.

"Come on," Kyla told her new friends. "I'll introduce you to Uncle Leath, and to Clyth." Eager to talk to the man wearing the sporran with the juniper cantle, the adults followed Kyla and Emily as they ducked under the barrier.

"Uncle Leath!" Kyla called once they were within hearing range. The man paused in his steps as he was walking off the field and turned toward his niece, holding out his arms. The girl launched herself into his arms, and he twirled her around.

"How did the *Seann Triubhas* go?" he asked as he set her feet back on the ground.

"Well enough to win," Kyla answered, her face flushed.

Emily interrupted the family moment. "Kyla was beautiful! I've never seen anyone dance like her!"

Leathan's dark eyes moved over to Emily. "And who might you be? You obviously know a little something about dance."

"Uncle, this is Emily Carson. She's a dancer too." Kyla reached over to pet the border collie sitting at her uncle's feet. "Em, this is my Uncle Leath."

Emily put her hand in Leathan's extended hand, where it was swallowed up in a friendly shake. "Why did you name your dog Clyth? What does it mean?" she eagerly asked, always curious.

A smile squinted in the man's eyes. "Clyth is the name of the place in Scotland where one of our ancestors lived in a castle."

"A castle?" Emily's voice squeaked a little. "A really and truly castle?"

"A really and truly castle," Leathan assured her. "It's not there anymore, but it was for many, many years."

Emily held a tentative hand out to Clyth, who sniffed it and then rubbed the side of his head against it. "You have a cool name, Clyth. Oh, and you're good with sheep too."

While the girls were distracted by the border collie,

the adults introduced themselves, explaining how they had met Kyla. Then Annie stepped closer to Leathan and pointed to his sporran. "Mr. Gunn, I'm interested in your sporran, and I'm hoping you can tell me a little about it. You see, I inherited my house in Stony Point from my grandmother—"

"And she's always finding the most puzzling things in her attic!" Peggy helped the story along.

Annie nodded at Peggy and continued. "Yes, I am. Recently I found a sporran, also sealskin like yours. But even more, its cantle is identical to yours. Since I have no idea where the sporran came from, and my grandparents never showed it to me, I'm trying to figure out if it held any significance to them, or if there's a story behind it." She paused, and then took the photo out of her purse and handed it to Leathan.

The man stood motionless as he gazed at the photo.

When he remained silent, Annie asked, "Do you know if the design on your cantle is unique to your family, the Gunns?"

Once again Leathan was still. Then he said quickly, "I don't believe it is, Mrs. Dawson. I'm sorry I can't help you."

Annie tried to hide her disappointment. "Please, do call me Annie. Don't worry about it. We've enjoyed getting to know Kyla a little, and the sheepherding was so exciting! Congratulations on your win."

"Thank you," Leathan nodded. Then he spoke to his niece. "Kyla, the other dogs are in their kennel. Come help me with them." Turning back to the others, he spoke to them. "Kyla and I need to go now. Enjoy the rest of the Games." Nodding briskly, he called Clyth to follow and put his arm around Kyla's shoulder to bring her along with him. Kyla waved over her shoulder and called, "Bye, Emily! It was nice meeting you!"

Startled at the sudden departure, the group from Stony Point stood looking at each other. They heard Kyla say to her uncle as he walked away from them, "Why do you need my help? Isn't Dev here?"

They couldn't hear Leathan Gunn's response.

12

The friends looked at one another, cocking their heads, perplexed. "We should probably be used to these unusual reactions by now," said Alice. "Especially Annie. But I'm not. How about the rest of you?"

Wally shook his head. "In my wild days I dodged trouble all the time, and well, sometimes trouble hit me right on the chin. But those were just consequences—you know? These folks are acting strange, for sure."

"Kyla's uncle wasn't mean," inserted Emily, not wanting her friend to be disliked by her family and adult friends.

Annie affectionately tugged the little girl's pigtails. "No, he wasn't, Emily. But he definitely was in more of a hurry to leave than he had been when he was telling you about his collie's name. I think he was bothered by the photo I showed him but didn't want to say it."

"I agree with Annie," said Peggy, "but before we decide what to do next, let's go gather our stuff." She glanced around at the new batch of contestants for the two-dog sheepdog finals gathering around the edge of the field. "We need to get off the field."

The group returned to the blanket. "Mom! Kyla left her dancing shoes!" Emily snatched up the black shoes and stood before Peggy, cradling them in her arms. "What should we do?"

Ian put on his mayor's fix-it tone. "Leathan said he needed Kyla to help with the dogs. All the kennels are kept in the same general area. We can go look around for her."

"Or maybe she'll go back to see some more of the dancing," added Alice, "*when* she gets done with the dogs." Alice's response made it clear she hadn't believed Leathan's claim that he needed Kyla's help.

Peggy finished folding the quilt and stuffed it into her bag. "So, why don't we first go to the kennel area and then try the dance stages, if Kyla's already gone?"

"And if we just can't find her, Emily, I'm sure they have a lost-and-found box somewhere," Annie told the anxious girl. "We can check the brochure for its location."

Emily's pigtails bobbed. "OK, Miss Annie. But can we hurry?"

The adults nodded as one, and they made sure they hadn't left anything behind. "Keep a good grip on those, Em," Peggy said, as though she didn't already know the girl was clutching the leather shoes as though her life depended on them. "Wally, which way to the kennels?"

Wally had been consulting the well-used brochure. He looked up, glanced around, and pointed to the left. "We need to head that way behind the first sheep pen and then around to an area near one of the parking lots. Let's go!" Map in hand, he started off, Emily walking beside him and the adults following.

Once they reached the grassy area dotted with dog kennels of many different sizes, the group split up to look for Kyla. The adults decided that whoever found her would text Wally to bring Emily and the shoes, hopefully without spooking Leathan.

But there was no need for texting. Kyla could not be found, and her uncle was not in the area either. They all met back at the designated place to proceed to Plan B, the dance stages. Those turned out to be much trickier to comb for one twelve-year-old dancer among the sea of kilted participants and crowds of spectators. Once again the group split into two, but before long they realized it was going to be nearly impossible to find Kyla in the crush of people. A text from Ian to Wally brought all the friends back together in front of Stage 3, the shoes still clutched in Emily's arms.

The girl's face showed her worry. "Does this mean we have to find the lost-and-found box and dump Kyla's shoes there?" From the tone of her voice, Emily felt as confident about the lost and found as animal lovers do about the pound. The adults looked around at one another. What was the best next step, for both Kyla and their favorite young dancer?

Annie drew in a slow and deep breath before offering her opinion. "There's still plenty of time left in the day, and with that is the chance we can see Kyla again. I see no reason why we can't keep the shoes with us while we do the other things we have planned. Then, if we don't see Kyla by four forty-five, we can leave the shoes with lost and found."

"Annie makes a reasonable suggestion," said Ian. "Does that sound good to you, Emily?" He turned to her, smiling gently.

Emily's arms tightened slightly around the shoes, but she nodded. "I want Kyla to know we took good care of them." Relief and lingering concern both played across her face.

"Em, if we do end up having to put Kyla's shoes in the

lost and found, we can tuck a note inside so Kyla will know how hard we tried to find her," Peggy told her daughter.

The little girl brightened, and she straightened her backbone, drawing her shoulders back. The dancer in her had found her balance again. "OK, Mom. I feel much better now."

"Since we have that decided, what should we do next?" Wally asked, his eyes still scanning the flow of people going by them.

Alice also kept watch for Kyla's sky-blue tartan as she replied, "The kilt-making demonstration starts soon. But I suspect you men would be bored."

Wally snickered. Ian grinned and answered, "Even though I wouldn't mind having some say in the kilt you ladies plan to make for me, I'll just have to trust your judgment. I've been thinking about the events of the day and what connections there could be between Hep the hammer tosser, the singer, and the falconer. Can we discuss it while Wally and I walk you to the demo building?"

Alice looked around at her girlfriends and answered for them all. "Yup. Let's walk and talk, as my father used to say."

"I've been thinking about the connections too, Ian," Annie confessed as they moved away from the dance platforms toward the building indicated on the map where the kilt-making class was to be held. "All the weird stuff started happening after we went through the vendor tents."

Peggy opened her mouth to speak, and then found she needed to step backward quickly to avoid colliding with a swerving baby stroller being pushed by a teenage girl. "Whoa, there!" Peggy blurted.

"Oops," the girl gasped. "Sorry!" The teen jerked the

stroller to the left to make more room and hurried away, her flip-flops smacking the ground like rapid fire.

Peggy's eyes followed the stroller for a moment. "I sure hope that girl doesn't harm the little one with her recklessness." She shook her head to refocus her thoughts. "Anyway, as I was about to say, Mr. MacTavish sounded like he'd been around the Games for a long time. He must know a bunch of the families that come every year."

"That's right," agreed Alice, "and he kinda paused when Annie showed him the ferrule, but he still said he didn't know which clan it was from. He even told us to try at the clan tents."

Annie snapped her fingers. "And yet, remember how the woman at Kilt and Caboodle told us right away that the ferrule had a custom design? Wouldn't someone who's been in the bagpipe business as long as Mr. MacTavish know it too?"

"Sounds suspicious to me," said Wally. He paused in his steps as the group came to an intersection of tents, glancing at the map once more. "We need to turn to the right here."

"Do you suppose Mr. MacTavish alerted Hep, and the singer, and Kyla's uncle about Annie's questions?" asked Alice.

Ian cupped his hand around Annie's left elbow to steer her over a few steps, making way for a pushcart of Highland Games paraphernalia moving past them. "Could be, Alice," he said. "Which gives me an idea of what Wally and I can do while you ladies learn kilt-making." He turned back to address Wally. "Why don't you and I go back to the athletic events and see what we can find out about Hep? Maybe we can have a longer conversation with him, if he's around."

Wally considered his friend's suggestion. "That's probably

the best thing we could do. But—" he paused and looked around at the women, "I won't be comfortable with Ian and me leaving you, unless you promise to stick together while we're gone." He gazed into his wife's eyes. "Peggy, no wandering off to follow some curious person or clue." Then he shifted his gaze back to the whole group. "And that goes for all of you."

"OK, Dad." Emily nodded sincerely, excited to be included in the group of women.

"What *she* said," Alice said with a wink over the girl's head.

Peggy's eyes glinted. "What if it's a totally safe clue?" When Wally pulled his shoulders back and opened his mouth to respond, she interrupted him. "I'm *kidding*! Don't go all bodyguard on me." She drew her arm through his and leaned into his side. "You know we won't do anything foolish with Em along."

Ian slowed down, peeking into the small building they had just approached. "This looks like the right building." He put on a stern face, wagging a finger in front of Annie and Alice. "Remember, you may have suckered me into wearing a kilt, but I'm still the mayor of Stony Point, and I will be representing our town. Keep that in mind as you choose the colors," he swallowed loudly, "and length."

The women chuckled. "Don't worry, Ian," said Alice. "We'll do you proud so you can do Stony Point proud."

Annie nodded her agreement and added, "Ian, we won't be making your kilt today anyway. We'll need to take your measurements first. You'll have a say in how the kilt is finished."

"Thank you," Ian responded, with as much dignity as he could muster. "If all goes well, perhaps I'll wear the kilt at the town's first Robbie Burns Dinner."

"Come on, Ian, stop yakking, and let's get a move on," Wally growled. "Maybe I'll still get to see some of the Sheaf Toss competition."

The females watched the two men stride away toward the athletic fields before entering the building. Peggy took Emily's hand and stepped through the doorway, and Annie and Alice followed.

Inside the single-room building, a woman stood behind a long white table filled with tartans and assorted sewing notions. Though her chin-length hair was a pure, soft white, the woman's skin was smooth with only small laugh lines at the corners of her cheerful eyes. She opened her arms wide in greeting to the newcomers.

"Come in, come in! We're just about to get started." She indicated some empty chairs closer to the table, and the Stony Point women quickly took their seats, smiling at the six other females gathered there. Emily stared at all the different tartan swatches mounted on a bristol board.

The woman began, "In case you've stumbled into the wrong building, I'm Brianna Kincaid, and I'll be demonstrating how to make your own kilt. If you were hoping to learn how to make Scottish black pudding, you've overshot by two doors." She waved her right thumb toward the right and looked around the group, as though waiting for someone to rise, but there were only snickers. "No pudding takers? Great! Let's get started."

Brianna picked up the bristol board that had captured Emily's attention. "Two of the foundational things you need to know before beginning a kilt are how to choose the best material and how to take correct measurements. On this board are just a few of the tartan patterns available. When choosing a tartan for a child, or a dancer, a kilt will look best if it's made using a pattern in proportion to the size of the wearer." The instructor pointed to three tartan patterns on the board. "These are examples of patterns suitable for an adolescent."

"Like me?" Emily asked. "I'm a dancer too!"

Brianna took the young girl's interruption in stride. "Yes, you would be the perfect size for these patterns." She touched the three choices once again. Peggy, Alice, and Annie all started to dig into their bags for notebooks and pens as quietly as they could. Noticing, the demonstrator told them, "I'll be handing out copies of the information I share today, along with resource pages. That way, you can watch what I do with undivided attention."

"Oh, thank you!" Alice said, gratefully. "I can imagine how funny my kilt would turn out if I missed writing down a step."

Brianna nodded in sympathy. "That's why I wrote up the notes. I'm a very visual learner and could never fully enjoy a demonstration when I was desperate to make sure I had not messed anything up while taking notes." All of the kilt-making students, including the group from Stony Point, relaxed in their seats.

Setting the board back on the table, the instructor picked up a stack of tartan squares. "Another thing you need to know about kilt material is that it comes in several different weights, such as super fine, lightweight, medium weight, heavy weight, and regimental weight." As she talked about the different weights of fabric, Brianna handed each student a set of tartan squares so they could feel the difference. After hearing the details of each weight, Annie made a mental note to herself that heavy-weight fabric would probably be best for Ian with his concern for being appropriately dressed for a public event like a Robert Burns dinner. Meanwhile, Peggy decided a lightweight fabric would be fine for Emily's kilt.

Next, Brianna showed them examples of different versions of some tartans. "This group is a wee bit familiar to me," she said, handing out four squares of tartan. Annie spread the four swatches on her lap. Green was the dominant color of two of the squares, while another used a wider band of black along with the green, giving it a darker look overall. The last square used tan as its background color. Annie stared down at the different renderings in fabric.

Brianna lifted one of the green squares. "This is the ancient Kincaid tartan." Exchanging it for the square with a brighter green, she said, "This one is the standard-color tartan." Next she held up one with a green so dark that, at a distance, it would be hard to see it contained both green and black with a thin red line. "This is what the modern colors look like. And last," she said as she exchanged the dark square for the tan one, "this is a reproduction tartan."

Peggy blinked at the last square. "What? That one doesn't look related to the others at all."

"It can get confusing," the instructor admitted. "Which is why I have listed the website addresses for both the Scottish Tartans Authority and the Scottish Register of Tartans on the resource pages I'll be giving you. You can look up any tartan on those sites."

"Oh, good. I'd never keep all those different tartans straight in my head," Peggy said. With her years of experience at The Cup & Saucer, Peggy could remember many special orders at a time, but all those variations of fabric made her head spin.

Setting the samples aside, Brianna turned next to the proper method of taking measurements for a kilt. When she emphatically declared one should not try to take measurements for oneself, both Peggy and Alice glanced slyly at Annie, who pretended not to notice. Apparently, somebody was going to have to measure Ian's waist—two inches above his navel—and his hips, and the length from his waist to mid-knee or above. Her friends made it clear to Annie who they expected the measurer to be.

An air of creative industry pervaded the tent as the group learned about pleating a kilt, what it meant to pin "to the sett" and "to the stripe," and the differences between different types of pleating. With her friendly, no-nonsense style of teaching, Brianna soon had her students recognizing knife pleats, box and double-box pleats, Kingussie and reverse Kingussie pleats, military box pleats, and tube pleats. Even Emily yelled out "Kingussie!" when the instructor held up an example and asked the group which pleat was used.

As their teacher gave tips for adding the lining to a kilt, Alice leaned over to quickly whisper to Annie and Peggy. "Brianna would be wonderful to have for a Hook and Needle Club event, don't you think?"

"Yes!" Peggy whispered back, while Annie nodded zealously.

"I'll ask her when the demo's over," Alice said, and then the three turned their full attention back to linings and waistbands. After a discussion on giving the kilt the finishing touches and some additional hints she had gathered over the years, Brianna wrapped up the demonstration.

She picked up a pile of stapled worksheets and began handing them out to the students. As she extended one toward Alice, Alice took the opportunity to ask, "Brianna, do you live in Maine?"

"Yes, I do," the instructor answered. "I live near Bath."

"We're part of a needlecraft club in Stony Point, and we were wondering if you'd be interested in doing an extended session for us?" Alice went on to explain about Ian's plan for a Robert Burns Dinner. "I think many people would be interested in learning how to make their own kilts, if the town board approves the mayor's idea."

Brianna put up a finger to ask for a minute and quickly handed out the rest of the worksheets, thanking each of the women for coming. Once the others had left the room, she returned to Alice and her friends.

"Stony Point, you said? That's not too far. I'd love to help." Brianna paused, thinking. "I've been toying with the idea of developing a needlecraft exchange. I could come help with kilt making or knitting, which is another love of mine, and your group could send someone to teach something to Bath's crafting community. Do you think your club would be interested?"

The three women looked at one another, trying to think like Mary Beth. "The club's leader is Mary Beth Brock, Annie said, "and while I can't speak for her, this sounds like something she would love to do. May we have your contact information?"

Brianna plucked some business cards from a stack on the table and handed one each to the three adults, giving Annie an extra one. "I do travel to several Highland Games around the country, but I'm sure we can easily work around them. I'll be looking forward to hearing from Mary Beth."

"Thank you so much," said Alice. "We really enjoyed your demo." She turned to her friends. "We'd better hurry. The guys will be wondering where we are."

They said their goodbyes to Brianna Kincaid and left the building, wondering what might come from the demonstration as they hurried to meet up with Ian and Wally.

13

"I hope Mary Beth likes the idea of the needlecraft exchange," Peggy said as she took Emily's hand.

Annie looked around her to make sure they were heading in the right direction for the athletic fields. "Can't you just picture Kate being a hit in Bath, sharing her amazing crochet designs?"

"Absolutely." Alice gave a quick nod. "And if the town board does approve the Robert Burns Dinner, I think we might increase our Hook and Needle Club membership with a kilt workshop."

"Stella might find that disconcerting," suggested Annie, "but I dare say she'd survive."

Alice chuckled. "The real question is will the newcomers survive Stella?"

"If I can survive as a transplant," Annie said, her smile turning into an outright laugh, "surely Stony Point natives will."

"With a little help from the rest of us," Peggy added. The sound of harp music diverted her attention. Looking around, she saw the source in a nearby building and pointed it out to the others. "Hey, I think we've found the harpers' building."

Emily snapped to attention at her mother's words. "Harpers'? Eli talked about that, didn't he, Mama?"

"Eli?" Alice asked.

"The fiddler without a kilt pin. I told you about him this morning," Peggy reminded her.

"Oh, that's right—the young lovebirds." Alice shook her head. "It feels like you told us the story months ago, instead of just this morning." The three women shared a rueful look amongst themselves.

"It's probably too early to see Eli and Linley, but do you mind if we just pop in for a quick glance around?" Peggy said, appealing to the romantic side of her friends.

"As long as you promise to be the one to explain to Wally and Ian why we took so long to meet them," answered Alice.

Annie added, "And we'll be fast—right?" She quickened her pace toward the sound of harps. Her friends followed her, Emily skipping in excitement.

Inside the long building stood a platform at one end bathed in fluorescent light. Five large harps and two smaller ones—behind which sat three women, two men, and two younger players who looked to be just into their teens—graced the platform. The younger players were not playing the current melody, but sat still with their hands in their laps. Though their hands were still, their torsos swayed almost imperceptibly to the music.

"I've always loved harp music," Annie whispered. "It sounds so otherworldly." She slipped into a seat in the last row, her friends filing in behind her.

Emily settled in next to her mother and immediately began to look around the room for any sign of Eli and his love interest. Like daughter, like mother, the movement of Peggy's head indicated she was doing the same thing.

After a few minutes, Emily leaned over to whisper, "I don't see them. Do you, Mom?"

Peggy was staring at the front rows, craning her upper body for a better look. Her eyes widened, and she turned to the others. "I don't see Eli and Linley either, Em. But I do see someone else." Alice and Annie raised their eyebrows in question. "The singer from the lunch tent!" She gestured in the direction of her gaze. "See her?" Their eyes followed Peggy's motion, and then they sat up a little straighter.

The tune finished with a gentle, lingering note, and the crowd appreciatively applauded. The woman harpist seated in the middle stood to introduce the next number, adding, "We are privileged to be accompanied for this next song by a woman with a voice of rare beauty. Please join me in welcoming McKenna Rose."

Applause again rang out, and the singer with the flowing light green and lavender dress slipped from her seat and glided up to the platform. As one, the friends in the back row changed from sitting erect to slumping in their seats, trying to ensure the crowd hid them from view.

"Should we slip out?" Peggy hissed through her teeth.

Annie and Alice both shook their heads. Annie mouthed, "After the song." The friends sat as still as they could while the chanteuse sang a haunting song of love and loss. Holding a long, tender note at the end of the song, McKenna Rose gave a regal bow to the harpists and then to the audience. Then, amidst the enthusiastic applause of the crowd, she once again slipped away through a back door.

As soon as the door closed behind the hem of the gossamer dress, Alice turned to her friends. "That woman has her disappearing act down just as well as her singing. I guess we don't have to slip out, after all."

"Do you suppose she saw us?" asked Peggy. "Here I thought we were doing such a good job slumping and all."

Annie shrugged. "Who knows? She wasn't staring at anyone like she did at the lunch tent." She dug her notebook out of her bag. "The harpist called her McKenna Rose, right?" She froze, the realization just dawning.

"Rose!" The three women exclaimed in unison, but quietly, as the harpists had begun their next, and final, tune. Annie wrote the name in bold letters and underlined it. "You don't suppose there is a connection between ...?" Annie whispered to her friends. She drew a line from McKenna's name to the falconer, Finley, floating a question mark beside it. "The hawk and rose design on the ferrules ...?" she whispered again. She showed the page to Alice and Peggy, who nodded, curiosity glinting in their eyes.

Meanwhile, Emily's eyes danced between the harpists' graceful hands and the two entry points of the long room as she sat mesmerized by the music, yet ever vigilant in case Eli might show. When the music ended, the friends stood to applaud along with the rest of the audience. Though distracted by the mystery of the sporran and ferrules, they still appreciated the delicate artistry of the musicians.

As their applause subsided, Emily tugged on her mother's arm. "Mom, can we stay a little longer? Eli might come, now that the music is done." She turned the voltage of her pleading eyes up a notch.

Peggy looked at the watch on her wrist. "I'm not sure,

Em." Turning to her friends, she asked, "What do you two think? Can we spare a couple more minutes?"

Alice was the first to answer. "Well, it's all right by me—I'm a sucker for young romance." They all turned to look at Annie.

"Don't look at me." Annie put her hands up like she was about to be arrested. "I love romance too, young or old or anywhere in between." She sat back down. "But let's just stay a few more minutes, or we might push Wally and Ian beyond what they can handle!"

Peggy grinned and sat back down as well, freely watching as people milled around the room, talking to the musicians or with each other. "Can't speak about Ian, but I've personally spent many years building Wally's patience level. What's the use of all my effort if I can't rely on it once in a while?"

"Well, we *are* following their advice by staying together," declared Alice. "What's a few minutes here or there?"

"Mom!" Emily interrupted the women's justification session with a whispered exclamation. "There's Eli!" The women followed the girl's line of vision and saw the slim fiddler hovering just inside the main entrance, scanning the people who lingered after the concert.

As they watched, the woman who had introduced McKenna hurried over to the young man, and they heard her say, "Eli! I'm so glad you're here! You can start stacking up the chairs. Uncle just left to get the truck for loading."

Eli nodded and began doing as his aunt had asked, but it was clear his mind was elsewhere. As he folded each chair, his eyes darted to the two doors, and once he even placed the chair he was stacking off-center, causing it to slide off the stack with a clatter.

"Oh, that poor boy," murmured Alice. "He's got it bad!"

Emily giggled. "I told you they were all googly-eyed."

Peggy took another look at her watch. "Googly-eyed or not, if Linley doesn't show up really soon, we're going to have to leave anyway," she warned her daughter. A furtive movement by the door caught her attention. "Hey, just in the nick of time. There she is!"

Emily clapped her hands, as though applauding the lead actors of a Broadway play. Annie and Alice looked in Linley's direction, trying not to be too obvious.

They could see that Eli was trying to play it cool, but he failed miserably. An ecstatic smile lit his face, and the chair under his hands collapsed to the floor as he rushed toward the entrance. His aunt looked up sharply at the noise, opening her mouth to correct her nephew. Realizing the cause of Eli's distraction, she kept silent and turned back to her own work with a gentle smile on her lips.

Annie turned to her friends. "As much as I'd love to stay and watch love bloom, we really need to go."

A guilty look crossed Peggy's face. "I know; you're right. At least we know Linley kept her promise to Eli. I hope we can come back next year and see if they're still googly-eyed."

The group slipped out of the building and into the flow of people using the door opposite of the one Linley had used. Annie barely heard the chime of her cellphone, alerting her of a new text message, over the din of the crowd. Digging it out of her bag, Annie unlocked her phone. The message read, "Is your demo done?"

"Hold up a minute," Annie told her friends. "Ian's asking if we're done, and I can't text and walk at the same time without it being gibberish." She stepped closer to a nearby tent so as to not block traffic as she tapped in her response, the others following her.

"Ask him where we should meet," said Alice. "They may have changed their minds about meeting at the beverage cart."

Annie typed, "Yes. Still meet at drink vendor?" After sending the message there was hardly time for her to close the phone before the chime rang again. She read Ian's response aloud. "No, come to athletic field A."

Alice pulled out her brochure and located the field. Looking around to make sure of their position, she pointed in the direction from where they had just come. "It's back that way, and at the main crossroads we need to turn right, and then left."

"Lead on, Alice." Peggy turned to her daughter and said, "Em, let me put Kyla's shoes in my bag. It's really chaotic here, and I'd feel better holding your hand. They'll be safe in here." She patted the large bag.

Emily was silent, the muscles of her face working. At last she nodded and handed her treasure to Peggy. Once the shoes were safely tucked away, she slipped her hand into her mother's, and the group hurried toward the field.

Annie spoke, her fast pace adding some huff to the words, "Do you think Ian asked us to come because they have new information?"

"If they do, then we've all had a very productive afternoon," answered Alice.

Peggy used her free hand to shove her bag more securely onto her shoulder. "Why else would they change our meeting place? Hey! Maybe they found someone in the Gunn or Rose family who's willing to talk!"

"Now, that would be amazing," Annie responded. "Though my mysteries rarely wrap themselves up quite so easily."

Alice laughed. "She's got a point, Peggy. But we can always hope."

"Wait a minute!" Peggy exclaimed. "That's too funny, especially since you and I were talking about classic rock music earlier, Annie."

"What do you mean, Peg?" Annie asked.

"Don't you get it?" Peggy laughed. "We're looking for the Gunns and the Roses. Get it? Gunns and Roses—like the rock band, Guns N' Roses!"

"Oh, good grief!" Alice interjected. She waved a hand at the intersection they were approaching. "This is where we turn right."

The women followed her around the corner. "How far until we turn left?" Peggy asked Alice, still snickering.

Alice squinted at the map in the bright sunlight, and then shaded it with her free hand. "Looks like there's an historic Highlands encampment where we need to turn. It's after the tents thin out." The ladies passed a Clan Campbell Society tent, and then a beer tent. As they continued on their way, the tents and small buildings were further apart, and the trees closer together.

"There's the encampment!" Annie exclaimed, anxious to hear what Wally and Ian had discovered. Just ahead, in the shade of several lush trees, was a makeshift tent—tan canvas material stretched over six poles, with only the two middle posts tall enough for a man to stand upright underneath the covering. In the corner stood a barrel—used as a table—and a rocking chair was nearby.

Outside the tent several men were gathered in a variety of dress representing different periods of Scottish history and positions in society. A man in red regimental coat and a Black Watch tartan kilt stood ramrod straight, a pipe dangling beneath his blond-gray mustache. As the women passed, he removed the pipe and acknowledged them with a bow. Only the twinkle in his eyes gave a hint as to his personality.

The Stony Point friends all nodded to him, directing a quick smile his way. Emily was more interested in another Highlander in shades of khaki and moss green, standing at ease with an old rifle at his side. Though his clothing may have been considered boring by a young girl, his hat was the object of her attention.

"Mom, is that a beanie he's wearing?" Emily had turned her face away from the man to ask.

Peggy nonchalantly ran her gaze over the entire encampment but made sure to get a look at the man her daughter indicated, especially the green hat festooned with a jaunty red feather. Then she bent close to answer, "It's called a tam-o'-shanter."

Emily grinned at the name. "That's a funny name! Why's it called that? I don't think Daddy would wear a hat with such a silly name."

"You're right, Em," Peggy said, chuckling. "He wouldn't wear that any more than he'd wear a kilt without pants."

She paused to think about her daughter's question. "Um, I don't know why it's called a tam-o'-shanter." She turned to Alice and Annie. "Do either of you know?" she asked.

Annie shrugged and shook her head, but Alice's face lit up. "I do, Em! Blame it on Robert Burns. More than two hundred years ago, he wrote a poem with a character named Tam. The hat's named for the poem, *Tam o' Shanter.*"

Emily considered the information Alice had just shared. Then she told them with a giggle, "If Mr. Mayor ever gets a border collie like Kyla's family, he should name it Tam."

"That's a brilliant idea, Em!" Annie told her. "Tartan and Tam have a nice ring to them." Seeing a pathway leading to the left, she turned to Alice. "Is this where we turn?"

Alice looked ahead of her to see if there were larger intersections close. Not seeing any, she answered, "This should be it. I guess the only way to find out is to take it and see where it leads." They turned onto the pathway, which wandered between two copses, providing them with a cooler walk in the shade for a while.

Before long, the trees gave way to a wide expanse of fields, perfect for athletic competitions. The first cordoned area was marked "Field A" in thick red letters. "Here we are. Good signage sure helps," Alice said as she started looking around for the men.

Peggy craned her neck to look over the spectators at the action on the field. Seeing a high horizontal pole set between two upright posts—like the ones used for pole vaulting—in the middle of the field, she smiled. "Looks like Wally got his wish about seeing some of the Sheaf Toss competition."

"Are you sure?" asked Alice. "They use those poles for

the weight throws too." She peered at the bar, noting its height. "Hmm, it's set pretty high. It probably *is* for the Sheaf Toss. The weight throws are quite a bit heavier than the sheaves. I doubt anyone could throw them so high."

As if to prove her right, the next athlete strode up to the apparatus with a pitchfork in one hand and a stuffed burlap bag in the other. Glancing up at the horizontal bar, he positioned himself between the two upright posts. Satisfied with his placement, he tossed the bag onto the ground.

"And here comes Jonno Forbes, attempting a personal best of thirty-five feet and three inches," the announcer's voice boomed with enthusiasm. The crowd cheered encouragement as the man stabbed the pitchfork into the bag and took a few deliberate steps away from the posts. His back to the bar, Jonno paused, took a deep breath, and then swung the bag sideways three times before jerking the fork upward and behind him to release the sheaf. It launched into the air. The women from Stony Point cheered with the rest of the crowd as the sheath arced perfectly over the bar with inches to spare.

As the man ran under the bar, his fisted hands raised in triumph, Annie turned to Peggy and said, "I can see why Wally didn't want to miss this. How fun to watch!"

"What you might not be able to tell from here is how heavy those sheaves are," Alice told her. "They weigh twenty pounds!"

Peggy's mouth formed an O. "That takes some serious muscle! Over thirty-five *feet*!"

"Did you see how he had room to spare?" Alice shook her head in wonder. "They could have set the bar even higher, and it still would have made it."

Familiar voices came from behind them. "Did you see that?" Wally blurted, too excited to bother with a greeting.

"Daddy, do they always toss the sheaf from behind their backs like he did?" Emily asked, hugging her father.

Wally wrapped his arms around his daughter. "Mr. Mayor and I have watched several so far, and they've all done it the same way."

"I'm glad we got here in time to experience it," said Annie. "Is Hep competing in this?" She looked first at Wally and then at Ian.

Peggy added, "Yeah—did you talk to him?"

The two men glanced at one another and broke into laughter. "No, Hep doesn't do the sheaf toss," Ian gasped in between guffaws.

Wally composed himself long enough to answer his wife's question. "Yes, we talked to Hep." He struggled to keep from more laughter.

The women stared at the two men as they let their laughter play out. Once the level of hilarity had lowered to the point of silly grins, all four females spoke in one unified voice.

"WHAT?"

14

"Sorry about that," said Wally, looking genuinely contrite. "Hep is a really funny guy."

"A funny guy who should probably make the switch to stand-up comedy and stay away from hefting heavy objects," Ian added. The puzzled female faces around him made Ian continue. "We'd better tell you the whole story."

Alice crossed her arms. "We would appreciate that." A collective and sympathetic groan sounded from the crowd around them as the bar fell off its perch, falling to the ground along with the sheaf. Shoulders slumping and pitchfork dragging the ground, the competitor slunk over to pick up the burlap bag.

"We might want to move away from the action," Ian suggested.

Wally surveyed their surroundings and then gestured behind Ian. "How about under those trees back there?" The friends relocated before taking up their discussion again.

"So Hep is funny but … ?" Alice prompted the men to continue their story.

Wally nodded. "We have some information from guys who have known him since he was a little kid. The funny part we could figure out for ourselves after talking with the man for a while."

"We'll take your word on the funny part, unless

Hep uses it to disarm folks—put them off their guard, you know." Annie pondered the possibility. "After all, it's pretty clear some of the folks here haven't exactly been forthcoming with their information. Some have probably outright lied."

Peggy set her bag down by her feet, where it slumped as though tired from the day's activities. "Yeah, like Mr. MacTavish. He seemed so nice, but he didn't say anything about the ferrule having a custom design." She paused. "Unless it was the vendor at Kit and Caboodle who wasn't telling the truth."

"I don't think Hep's like that," Wally declared. He looked at Ian for collaboration.

Ian wiped his forehead. "In politics you either learn to read people, or you can't serve them. My gut instinct agrees with Wally about Hep. Especially after hearing stories from some of the other athletes."

"What did they say?" asked Alice.

Before answering, Ian asked if they would all like to sit down. Peggy answered, "Nah, we sat at the kilt demo and at the harpers' building, and we have the ride home. I'd rather stand." The other women showed their agreement with Peggy, and since Emily was always moving, her preference was a given.

"Harpers' tent?" Ian's eyebrows raised.

Annie waved off the mayor's question. "We'll tell you about that later. Finish telling us about Hep first."

Wally picked up the story. "When Ian and I first got to the field, the Heavy Weight for Distance contest was just about to begin. As we looked around, we saw the entire perimeter completely covered with people." He looked around at the ladies. "Remember how the whole corner was free when we went to watch the Hammer Throw event?"

"How could we forget?" Alice snorted. "Our choice to watch from that area sure made for an eventful morning."

"While we were wedging ourselves into the only space we could find," Wally continued. "It was about the size of a toolbox, and Ian made a comment about the wide open space we'd found at the Hammer Throw. A couple of guys standing to the left of us heard us and started laughing."

A small scowl creased Peggy's forehead. "Laughing before they knew what had happened? It wasn't funny thinking my friend might have been mowed down by that hammer."

Wally drew his arm around his wife's shoulders and gave her a squeeze. "Peg, they weren't at the Hammer Throw round. They were doing one of the other events, so they didn't know what had happened. But they did know Hep real well."

Ian continued the story. "One of the men trains at the same club that Hep does. Apparently, Hep has a beautiful hammer throw almost year-round … until he steps on the field for the Highland Games. For the last five years, Hep has choked and released the hammer too soon." He paused to clear his throat. "Seems Hep always launches at that particular corner, so the folks who are regulars don't stand near there."

"Why don't they put a sign up or something, so newcomers aren't put at risk?" Alice demanded, putting her hands on her hips. "I can't imagine it being good for business if someone got hurt."

Wally rushed to explain. "Bart—that's the training buddy of Hep's—told us the regulars like Hep so much they don't want to risk making him even more nervous by blocking off the area. They fear it might make Hep up and quit completely, and they want to see him finally succeed some year."

"When we told them about what happened to Annie, they were appalled," Ian inserted. "Both of them promised to work with the organizers and come up with a solution before next year so it doesn't happen again."

As the story gained momentum, the two men alternated information. "Hep worked his way through the crowd to stand next to his training buddy and recognized us," added Wally.

"He apologized to us again," said Ian. "He asked if you were still feeling all right after your fall."

"You mean after her being flattened by her bodyguard," Peggy corrected him, grinning.

Annie blushed softly and wagged a finger at her friend. "And what would have happened to me if Ian hadn't flattened me?" She shuddered. "I have too many vegetables that need tending to waste time with a concussion or broken bone."

Giving his wife a swift look to see if she was about to reply, Wally took over. "The weird thing is that Hep started talking to us about his hammer trouble at the Games, and he has it all analyzed down to the exact degree angle he was off on his release this morning. It's like he's a trigonometry major or engineer."

"After talking to Hep, I'm looking forward to coming

next summer and cheering him on," said Ian. "Just from a different vantage point."

Alice stood, quietly turning over the facts in her mind. "Did you happen to find out if Hep is from the Gunn or Rose clan?"

Both men looked her way with puzzled faces. "Rose?" they asked in unison. Ian added a question. "Because of the rose on the ferrule?"

"No," Annie answered. "Because we discovered the singer's name when we stopped at the harpers' building after the kilt demonstration. You know, Ian. The flirty singer from earlier today."

Emily had been watching two birds in the tree above them, but the mention of the singer reclaimed her attention, and she jumped into the conversation. "Her name is McKenna Rose! I think her name is as pretty as her dress!"

"Her name also tells us she might be connected to whoever had those ferrules engraved," Ian said, putting the pieces of information together, "which makes her behavior earlier a little more understandable—perhaps."

Emily wasn't done yet. "Mr. Mayor, we also saw Eli and Linley!" The sparkle in her eyes broadcasted her joy at the fact.

"Eli and Linley?" Ian squinted at her, puzzled. "Who are they?"

Peggy answered, "They're two cute teenagers in a budding romance." Her eyes flickered between the mayor and Annie. "Em and I first saw them in one of the kilt accessory tents, which Linley's parents own. Then they showed up at the harpers' building ... but we couldn't stay long enough to see what happened between them." She drew in a breath and let it out in an exaggerated sigh to her daughter's delight.

Wally turned to his wife. "Are these kids a part of any families who might be involved in the mystery?"

She shrugged. "We never heard any last names. We're not exactly in the Victorian age anymore, you know. Kids don't address each other as Miss This or Mister That."

"Peggy, do you remember the name on the vendor's tent?" asked Alice.

"It was a punny one, so yeah, I remember it," answered Peggy. "It's called Dress to Kilt." She paused. "I'm trying to remember if there were any signs inside the tent about the owners or any permanent shop they run but … ." She raised her hands and then let them drop in helplessness.

"We do know Eli's aunt is one of the harpists," said Annie, sending a compassionate glance to Peggy.

"And possibly the leader, as she was the one who introduced McKenna when she sang that one song with them," Peggy added. "It never occurred to me the kids or the harpist might be connected to the mystery, so I never tried to find out her name."

The two men stood silent for a time, taking in the new information. Then Ian asked, "Did you try to talk to McKenna? Or did she run off again when she saw you?" A mighty cheering rose up from the spectators watching the event behind them.

"We tried really hard to be inconspicuous," Annie told the men. "After what happened at the food tent—once we knew her name—we figured the best thing to do was just to watch."

Peggy finished the tale. "But she did glide right out of the tent as soon as she finished the song—no sticking around until the end of the set. Can't figure out if she's socially inept, a diva, or one of those whackadoo creative folks."

"We may never figure out the reasons behind her behavior, but we're certainly going to try," Alice declared. "That will be considerably easier since we now have her name."

"Sure, we might be able to find her address," Wally said, "but that doesn't mean she'll ever answer the phone or letter or email or whatever else we use."

"I agree that attempting direct contact might not be the most effective method," Ian said. "Using some messenger she likely knows, or at least would be less likely to shun might work better."

Annie thought about Ian's suggestion. "Sounds like a good idea to me, but how do we know who she actually knows? There were those two burly guys stationed at the exit of the dining tent where she was singing at noon, but I can't see them playing currier."

"How about Eli's aunt, for a start?" said Peggy.

"It must have been either Mr. MacTavish or the woman at Kilt and Caboodle who tipped off McKenna and the falconer," Alice reminded them. "If we leave a message with either of them, do you think there's any chance it will go anywhere but in the trash?"

The group grew quiet, each one thinking over the

situation, and Emily's attention went back to the birds and their nest.

Ian shrugged. "I don't see that we have any choice but to try it. McKenna may never get it, but then again she might. All we're wasting is a bit of paper and time. That's a minimal investment from my point of view."

The rest of the adults agreed with the mayor's idea, and Annie pulled out her notebook and pen to write the note.

"OK, so I'll write something like: 'Dear Ms. Rose, I have come into possession of a sealskin sporran and silver bagpipe ferrules engraved with a hawk and rose design. I believe they may belong to someone from either the Gunn or Rose family, and I want to return them to their rightful owner. If you know who that may be, please forward my contact information to the appropriate person or people. My address is —'"

Ian held up a hand. "Annie, I don't want you to give your home address or number and open yourself up to the possibility of harm. Please let me be the contact at Town Hall." He glanced around the group for their reactions to his plea. Annie paused in her writing to gauge the response of her friends.

"I second the motion!" Alice said, immediately giving her approval to the idea, while Wally and Peggy both nodded with enthusiasm.

Annie surrendered to the common sense of her friends. "I see your point, Ian, and appreciate your willingness." She drew a line through the last sentence she had started and exchanged Ian's name, position, address, and the phone number of Town Hall. "Did I leave anything out?"

Peggy ticked off the necessities with her fingers. "One: sporran, two: ferrules with hawk and rose, three: Gunn or Rose family, four: plea to give the information to owners, five: Mr. Mayor's address and phone number—sounds like everything important to me."

"How many copies of the request should Annie write?" asked Alice. "I think one should go to Leathan Gunn."

"And one to Finley the falconer," added Wally, "even if we don't know his last name. What happened after lunch makes it pretty obvious he's involved somehow." He turned to Ian. "Maybe it would be easier to get it to Brooke and ask her to deliver it to Finley."

Ian nodded his agreement with the idea. "If he's trying to keep things under wraps, I should think Brooke would be more effective as a messenger than any of us."

When Emily noticed Annie writing her notes, she ran over to Peggy and added, "Mom, I should write the note to Kyla now. We can't forget about her shoes!"

"Sure, Em." Peggy rummaged around her bag and found the pad of drawing paper she had brought in case her daughter got bored during the car ride. "After we write the message, we'll figure out how to get it to her uncle."

Emily's face brightened. "What should we write?" She sat down with the pad and pen, her mother at her side in case she needed help with the note.

Annie finished the three messages. "I'm going to write two more messages—one for Mr. MacTavish and the other for the vendor at Kilt and Caboodle, in case there's someone else who needs the information, someone we may not know about yet." She flipped to the next page and started writing again.

"If we don't hear from anyone, at least we'll know we did our best," Alice said. She moved over next to Emily, who had finished the note to Kyla and now had colored pencils for illustrating it—first adding some purple and pink lupines, and then with black shoes, *en pointe* between the blooms. "That's really pretty, Em," Alice said.

Emily's tongue slipped between her lips as she completed the ribbons on the shoes, just so. She looked over her artwork, and then nodded in satisfaction. "Thanks, Miss Alice. I hope Kyla likes it too." She handed the paper to Peggy.

"How could she not?" said her mother, smiling over the words and pictures. "She'll be thrilled to have her shoes back too." She carefully folded the note into a tidy rectangle small enough to slip into the shoes. Pulling one of the black shoes out of her bag, she tucked the paper inside before settling it back into its nest.

Annie signed the last of the notes. "There! All done." She bent over the notebook as she tore the papers out along the perforated lines. Handing them to Alice, she proceeded to pack away the book and pen.

While the ladies had been focused on the note writing and decorating, Wally had been keeping an eye on the Sheaf Toss competition. He jerked a thumb toward the field. "Hey, if you're all done with the notes, we should probably start back to the vendors. It looks like the last couple of guys are doing their final toss, and there will be a stampede from here in a couple minutes."

Alice quickly folded the last note. "Let's go then." The six friends walked out from under the shade of the trees and followed the path toward the main thoroughfare.

When they reached the Highlanders encampment, Emily pointed out her favorite hat to Wally. "Daddy, see the hat with the red feather? It's called a tam-o'-shanter, all because of Robert Burns." She waved at the man, who lifted his gun and saluted the young girl with it.

"That Robert Burns guy sure did get around," said Wally, grinning down at his daughter. He drew his eyes back to the men at the encampment. "Gotta feel a little sorry for the guys with the heavy wool uniforms. They must get mighty hot some days, standing out in the summer sun."

"Especially if they travel south to other Highland Games," exclaimed Annie. "I can't imagine wearing that during a Texas August!" She fanned herself at the thought.

Ian looked slyly over at Wally. "You have to admit, Wally, wearing a kilt would be cooler in the South."

"Ayuh," came the response from Wally's perfectly straight face. "That's another reason I'm just fine with staying put where I was born."

Laughing, the friends continued on their way, Emily peering through the throngs of people on the chance she might still find Kyla. But by the time they had all reached MacTavish's tent, the shoes were still in her mother's possession. Noticing how her shoulders were drooping with disappointment, her father whispered to her, "Em, you stay outside the tent with me, and we'll keep looking while the others deliver the messages. OK?" Hearing her husband's suggestion, Peggy handed her daughter the dancing shoes.

Cradling the shoes in one arm and slipping her free hand into her father's strong grasp, Emily nodded. "Thank you, Daddy." They stepped close to the tent canvas, out of the way of the foot traffic as the others entered MacTavish's, but their eyes roamed diligently over the crowd, looking for the sky-blue kilt and the graceful movement of the young dancer.

They had been standing beside the tent only five minutes when their friends joined them. "Was MacTavish there?" Wally asked.

"Yes," answered Ian, "and he did take two of the notes from Annie."

Annie added, "He didn't actually confess to knowing McKenna, but he did take the note addressed to her and promised to 'try to locate her.'"

"I hope MacTavish was telling the truth this time," said Peggy. "Do you think we should take the note to Eli's aunt now?"

Alice glanced up from the map she had been consulting. "You know, the lost and found booth is close to the harpers' building. Peggy, why don't you, Wally, and Emily deliver both the note and the shoes? The rest of us will stop at Kit and Caboodle, and then we'll look for Brooke to give her Finley's note."

Peggy took a glance at her watch and nodded. "It *is* getting pretty close to closing time. We don't want to keep the shoes so long that Kyla doesn't have time to ask about them at the lost and found." Seeing

Emily hug the shoes closer, Peggy gently patted her daughter's shoulder.

A frown lowered the corners of Emily's mouth, but she slowly nodded. "I know, Mom." She sighed. "I just wish we'd seen her."

"Me too," said Peggy. "But I wrote our address in the note, in case Kyla wants to write. Maybe you'll see her dance again next year." Deciding where they would meet the others after their errands were completed, the Carsons entered the stream of people, which was starting to thin as parents carried their mementos and tired children to the parking lot.

Thirty minutes later, every note duly entrusted to messengers they didn't know, the Stony Point friends followed the crowd leaving the Highland Games.

15

Annie nestled into the cushioned deck chair at Grey Gables, luxuriating in the soft breeze that flowed across her front porch. After her jam-packed Saturday at the Highland Games, she intended to take her Sunday as a serious day of rest. On the small round table beside her stood a glass of iced sweet tea next to a stack of her grandfather's journals.

As soon as she had returned from attending the morning worship service at Stony Point Community Church and had eaten lunch, Annie had combed through the multitude of journals Charles Holden had composed and saved during his many years as a veterinarian. Lining the bottom shelf in Grey Gables's library, the journals were arranged in chronological order, which made the task of finding the ones most likely to contain what Annie was looking for simple. She started by selecting the journals labeled 1978, the year the Highland Games had begun, to 1985.

She paused to gaze at the seascape before her. Few things moved her as much as the sight of the ever-changing water world. At times, it terrified her with its power and anger. Often, as on that warm August day, it soothed and delighted her. Always, it seemed to put things into perspective.

Annie stretched her arms overhead just in time for Boots to spring onto her lap and nose around under her chin. Lowering her arms, she returned the favor by caressing the cat in the same location. "Did you miss me yesterday, Boots?" After a "meow" and some kneading with her paws, the feline answered by curling up in a tidy heap in Annie's lap and making herself comfortable.

"I'll take that as a yes." Smiling, Annie reached over and plucked the first journal from the pile. "Hope you don't mind being a book rest." Positioning the soft-backed book on the cat, she opened to the first page. As always, the sight of her grandfather's handwriting brought both poignancy and comfort. How she missed her parents and grandparents! How thankful she felt to have so many reminders around her of the people they had been, and the ways in which they had helped her to grow into the woman she was.

Annie began to read, her movements limited to page turning, tea sipping, and the occasional cat scratching. Transported back to 1978, she experienced the workdays—and sometimes nights—of a country veterinarian through her grandfather's eyes, each one different from the one before it. In comparison, her years of bookkeeping for the car dealership had been decidedly more staid, although not without their own charms.

Ninety minutes later she was chuckling over an incident between her grandfather and a woman "bent on poodlizing the entire town" when Alice's voice surprised her from the other side of the porch. "What's so funny?"

"Oh! You startled me." Annie ran a hand over Boots's head to apologize for interrupting the cat's nap with her jerky movement. She raised the journal for her friend to see while Alice climbed the porch steps. "One of Grandpa's journals," Annie explained. "He truly had a way with words."

Alice crossed the porch and sat in the chair on the opposite side of the table from Annie. "People don't always write the way they talk, but Charlie certainly did." She surveyed the stack of journals. "Looking for Gunns or Roses?"

"Either or both, I guess," Annie replied. "And no, I haven't found any yet, but I'm only up to 1980." Annie passed the open journal over to her friend. "Here—read this story while I start the next one. You'll get a kick out of it." Noticing Alice's eyes on her almost empty glass of tea, she added, "Would you like some sweet tea while you read?"

"Subtle, aren't I?" said Alice. "I'd love some, but I hate to interrupt Boots's nap there."

Annie waved a hand, as if swatting the guilt away like a fly. "Neither of us has moved for an hour and a half. We could both stand to interrupt our inertia long enough for me to pour us some tea."

"After yesterday, you have earned some inertia time. Though I suspect Boots had plenty of it while you were gone." Alice reached over to rub the cat's ears. "Why don't you go chase mice or bugs from Annie's garden, lazybones?" One feline eye opened into a slit for a moment before closing again. "Or maybe not."

Chuckling, Annie picked up Boots as she stood to go get the sweet tea, and then she unceremoniously deposited the cat on the vacated cushion. After watching the woman who had put an abrupt end to nap time pick up her glass and head for the door, the feline stuck one leg out and began to groom.

"Ruffled your fur, did she?" Alice murmured before

turning her attention to the journal in her hand. By the time Annie pushed open the door with her shoulder, two frosty glasses in her hands, Alice was grinning from ear to ear.

"Here you go." Annie extended a glass toward her friend. "Funny isn't it?"

"It's even funnier because I remember this woman! Charlie captured her in perfect detail. She tried to convince my mother we needed to add a poodle to our household."

Annie reclaimed her chair and took a sip. "Did it work?"

"Oh, no!" Alice laughed. "She nearly had Mother convinced, but I threatened revolt. You know, I never liked poodles. And for once, my sister, Angela, agreed with me, so Mother changed her mind." She lifted the glass to her lips, sipped it and then exclaimed, "Wow, this is sweet!"

Annie raised an eyebrow. "Yes, dear, that's why they call it *sweet tea*. It's also why I only drink it during the warm days of Maine summer."

"Good thing you're not the couch-potato type," Alice declared. "You must burn it off during your high-energy mornings." She handed the journal back to Annie and gestured at the remaining pile. "Do you want me to start on 1981?"

Annie plucked the top book from the stack and held it out to her. "Yes! Just make sure you tell me if you find anything really hilarious, or anything about the Gunns or Roses, of course." She paused a moment. "Do you think anyone will ever contact Ian?"

Alice laid the journal in her lap and took another sip from her glass. "Who knows? People often don't make sense, in case you haven't noticed."

"And those folks seem so tightly knit," pondered

Annie. "Even more than people in Stony Point when I first came back."

Alice was quiet as she thought of the moment she and Annie first saw each other again when Annie was unloading her car after inheriting Grey Gables from Betsy. They had put in a lot of work reconnecting after decades. "Hard to believe, isn't it?" Alice asked "Especially when you think of the first Hook and Needle Club meeting you attended."

Annie rolled her eyes, but a smile hovered around her lips. "Now that you mention it, Leathan reminds me a little of Stella."

Alice looked sideways at her friend until they both started giggling. After catching her breath, she said, "To anyone else, you would sound absolutely crazy, but I get it." She sighed and looked out at the sea, as Annie had earlier. "I'd love for us to discover the story behind the sporran and ferrules. Is there anything else we can do besides look through Charlie's journals?"

"I haven't thought of anything else yet," Annie answered. "Maybe someone else will come up with an idea at the next club meeting."

Alice nodded. "Sometimes a little distance helps to see a challenge from a different slant."

"Speaking of challenge, I wonder how Gwen is surviving her bank weekend." Annie opened the journal in her hand. "The next meeting promises to be filled with stories."

"Hopefully, it'll be filled with some successful brainstorming too." Alice followed her friend's example and turned to the first page of the 1981 journal. "Although I think we can cut Gwen a little slack if her brain is numb."

"Agreed." Annie checked the time on her watch. "Let's read for an hour, and then I'll make us some dinner—maybe some pasta salad with my garden veggies and grilled chicken."

Alice's eyes brightened. "Sounds delicious." She lowered her eyes to the book in her hands. "I'm glad I forgave you for losing touch. Who knew you'd turn out to be such a good cook?"

"Right back at you, Muffin Maven," Annie said, smirking, before settling her concentration back to the last month of 1980. The banter put aside, the two women managed to skim through the rest of the journals through 1985. Though they found many amusing stories of wayward animals and curious people, they did not find any Gunns or Roses.

Alice plunked the 1985 journal onto the top of the stack. "How much further should we read?"

"There's only a few more left," answered Annie. "Grandpa was pretty much retired by 1990, although he was always helping out whoever needed it, according to Gram's letters." She stretched her arms overhead and arched her back. "I'll glance through them later, before bed. I need a break from reading for a while. Want to help me snap some green beans for dinner?"

Alice stood up, gathering the stack of journals in her arms. "Sure. I'll put these back in the library first. Should I grab the last of the journals for you while I'm there?"

"That would be great. Thanks!" After picking up the two empty glasses, Annie followed her friend into the house. "Just put them on the table in the hall. I'll get the beans ready for snapping." Once inside, the women parted for different rooms of the house, but they were soon reunited in the kitchen with a bowl of fresh green beans between them.

Alice glanced over at the harvest basket, piled with green cucumbers three to four inches long, on the counter next to the sink. "Did you pick all those cukes this morning?"

Annie snapped the ends off the bean in her hand. "Yes, I did. And there's more from yesterday morning in the mudroom. If I don't do something soon, I'm going to run out of room!"

"Sounds like pickling time to me," Alice hinted, as she picked up a bean. Boots padded into the room and crouched next to her water dish for a drink.

"You'll be happy to know it's on my to-do list for tomorrow." Annie gestured at a bowl of garlic bulbs sitting in the center of the table. "As you can probably tell from all the garlic, I'm starting with dill. Then I'll try bread-and-butter pickles. But I have some bad news."

Alice tossed a snapped bean onto the growing pile and raised an eyebrow.

"Reading over Gram's recipes, I realized my pickles won't be ready for the Labor Day picnic." Annie frowned at the bean in her hand. "Not by a long shot."

Alice thumped her hand down on the table. "I totally forgot about that! They have to sit and soak in all the tasty flavors, right? Just make sure you put some jars aside for next year."

"Do you mind waiting for a couple months before receiving your pay for helping me in the garden?"

Her friend sighed with an air of martyrdom. "If I must." She reached over to finger one of the bulbs of garlic. "It'll be worth it, if you follow Betsy's method to the letter. Over the years I ate a truckload of her pickles, and never once did I bite into a mushy one."

"From what I read in Gram's notes, the key is soaking the cucumbers in an ice bath for at least two hours as well as starting with firm cucumbers." Annie nodded at the harvest basket. "Those feel just right to me. What do you think?"

Alice finished snapping the ends off a green bean and added it to the bowl before sauntering over to where the day's harvest was nestled. She gently tested the feel of the cucumbers. "They feel just right, Annie. If they end up mushy, it won't be the vegetables' fault."

"Thanks—I think." Annie frowned, only half joking. "How come I suddenly feel like the entire success of next year's Labor Day picnic is riding on me following Gram's recipes perfectly?"

Alice returned to the table and looked her childhood friend in the eyes. "Don't you think you might be taking too much responsibility onto yourself?" Placing a hand on each of Annie's shoulders, she gave Annie a little shake and grinned. "Just say no to perfectionism! Seriously, do you really want your identity to be wrapped up in *pickles*?"

Annie's shoulders relaxed under Alice's hands. "It does sound pretty silly, since you put it that way." A quick shadow of embarrassment flitted across her face. "I loved Gram so much, but sometimes—the way folks talk—it seems like she *was* perfect. The shining example of the Proverbs 31 woman—I doubt I could ever live up to her legacy."

"Who ever said you had to?" Alice asked. "Her legacy is hers, and yours is yours. Besides, you have talents Betsy never had. There's a reason Charlie had someone else doing the financial record keeping for his and Betsy's businesses. Does that mean you're better than your Gram because you rocked at bookkeeping for the dealership? Or do you ever feel like you should be a missionary like your parents?"

Annie shook her head. "I never did feel any pressure to follow in my parents' footsteps. For some reason, it was easier to realize I wasn't called to missions than it has been for me to embrace being different from Gram. Maybe it's because I always saw her as a kindred spirit, being more of a homebody like she was."

"That's OK as long as you remember you are her granddaughter, not her clone," Alice said, wagging a bean at her friend.

Annie resumed her bean snapping. "Point taken. How'd you get so smart?"

"It's always easier dealing with someone else's emotional baggage than with your own," Alice replied. "But in this case, it's terrain I've traveled for decades, thanks to my own family's legacy."

"And you've done a pretty good job of being who you are all these years, in spite of it." Annie smiled at her friend. "I know it was really tough on you going through your divorce. I wasn't here for you then, but I know Gram was. I have always been thankful she was. Thanks for using your struggle to help me with mine." She plucked the last bean from the bottom of the bowl. "Now it's time to cook these beauties."

"Good. I'm getting hungry." Putting aside both the blessings and challenges of family legacies, the two women turned their attention to more immediate concerns, like cooking dinner.

Several hours later, the sun had gone down, and Alice had returned to her cozy carriage house. Annie opened her bedroom windows a little wider to let in more of the cool summer night air. The wonder of enjoying August nights free of air-conditioning never seemed to wane for her, and she stayed at the window for a while, simply letting the breeze move around her. By the time she turned away from the window, Boots had already claimed her patch of the patchwork quilt on the four-poster bed.

Annie collected the next veterinarian journal, 1986, from the short stack where she'd placed it on her bedside table and nestled into her comfortable chair. Opening the cover, she pictured her grandfather with that spark of latent mischief in his eyes as he sat at the rolltop desk in the library after each workday, scribbling his observations. The flow of his writing and the images he described reminded her of the bedtime stories he told her during her childhood summer visits.

"Here I am, a grandmother, and you're still telling me bedtime stories, Grandpa. Thank you," she murmured. Turning to the next page, a name jumped out at her—Mitchel Gunn. He apparently had needed Doc Holden's help with a sheep that was suffering from a large abscess on his neck. Reading through the note, thankful it did not contain photos of the procedure, Annie's eyes grew wider at the end. Her grandfather had written, "The sealskin goes to the one who bears the falcon and the rose."

With a little squeal, Annie lunged for the phone, not bothering to check how late it was. Alice never went to sleep earlier than Annie.

"Hello?" Alice answered.

"I found it!" Annie exclaimed. "It was in 1986. Grandpa went to the farm of a Mitchel Gunn to help with a sheep."

"Could Mitchel be related to Leathan Gunn?" Alice asked, her excitement obvious in her voice.

Annie looked down at the page. "There's no mention of Leathan, but Grandpa did make a very interesting notation at the end. He wrote, 'The sealskin goes to the one who bears the falcon and the rose.'"

She heard Alice gasp over the phone line. "Thank you, Charlie! Is there an address of the farm in the entry?"

"No, just that it was the Mitchel Gunn farm."

There was silence on the line for a moment. "Farms usually stay in families, around here, for generations and generations. If the Gunn farm is close enough for Charlie to vet for, it shouldn't be too hard to track down. I wouldn't be surprised if Leathan answers the door once we find it, either."

"Not if he sees us coming," said Annie. "First, I'll see if I can dig up any additional records with an address or phone number from Grandpa's papers. If I can't find anything, then before the club meeting on Tuesday, I'll stop at the library and see if I can find out where the farm is located." She paused, staring out the window as she thought. "Even if I do find the Gunns' address, I think I'm going to wait a few weeks before I try to contact the family."

"Why?" Alice sounded puzzled.

"You saw how Leathan reacted after seeing the photo of the sporran. If I show up so soon after that, assuming he is related to Mitchel and lives at the same farm, my chances of him talking to me are pretty much nil."

A disappointed sigh came to Annie's ear. "You're right," Alice muttered. "I shouldn't complain. We've only been back from the Games one day, and already we have an additional lead. Not too shabby."

"Not shabby at all," her friend agreed. "And since we have accomplished so much today—and I have a horde of cucumbers to pickle tomorrow—I'm going to say goodnight and go to bed."

"Sleep well, early bird," Alice told her. "Let me know if you need any help tomorrow. I've left the day completely unscheduled."

A smile touched Annie's lips. "I will, and I'll try not to need help too early."

Alice chuckled. "It took a while, but I've finally got you trained. Have good dreams."

"You too—when you finally tumble into bed." The friends ended their call.

Standing at the foot of her bed, Annie scratched her cat under the chin before getting ready to climb into bed. "It's the end of an exciting weekend, Boots. What will the coming week bring?"

The cat's mouth opened in a wide yawn. Whatever was coming, Boots wasn't going to face it without plenty of sleep. Annie intended to follow her example.

16

A couple of weeks later, Annie stood in front of her stove stirring a concoction of two different kinds of vinegar, sugar, mustard seeds, turmeric, cloves, garlic, and some dried chopped cayenne peppers in a saucepan. As she waited for it to boil over the high heat, she turned to check the view from the window. The landscape was still gray with fog. Although Maine was known around the country for its nor'easters, Annie had been reacquainted during the summer with the "smoky sou'westers" she had experienced during her childhood visits at Stony Point. Those were days when a friendly southwestern wind pushed the morning fog off the coast and onto the outer banks. Having planned to go into town with Alice for lunch at The Cup & Saucer, she hoped the fog would burn off—or blow out—by noon. Sometimes it did. Sometimes it didn't.

The sound of the mixture bubbling into a boil directed Annie's attention back to her pickling. This week she was making a sweet and spicy recipe. Annie reduced the heat under the saucepan and reached for the bowl of sliced onions and cucumbers which she had already soaked for a couple of hours and drained. She shook the vegetables into the pan and gently stirred them into the mixture with a wooden spoon. Humming, she waited until the contents of the saucepan were simmering and then removed it from the heat, switching off the burner with the quick flip of her hand.

Since the day of the Highland Games, Annie had kept busy in her garden. She now had a small army of jars filled with dill pickles, relish, and summer squash decorating the shelves of her bakers rack. Earlier in the morning, as she had circled a date on her calendar, the day on which she planned to mail the garden goodies to her family, she realized how much time had passed since delivering those handwritten messages to Mr. MacTavish and the others. It was looking more and more like she'd have to use the information Grace had helped her find at the library if she was ever to discover the story behind the sporran and ferrules. But with the fog, she wasn't going to head out to unknown roads just yet. She'd be pleased simply to be able to find the diner in town instead of ending up in the harbor.

Selecting a slotted spoon from the collection of utensils sprouting out of a stoneware crock, Annie divided the cucumbers and onions between the hot, sterilized pint-size jars lined up on the counter next to the stove. Pouring carefully, she filled each jar with enough of the liquid to reach up to a half-inch from the top. After trading the spoon for a towel she had dampened, she made sure each rim was clean and then fit each jar with a lid.

Annie had just placed the jars into a hot-water bath when the phone rang. Setting a timer first, she grabbed the phone from the charger. "Hello?"

Ian's crisp, friendly voice responded, "Good morning, Annie. Are you busy? I have some news for you."

"Well, I have about fourteen minutes until I need to take my pickle jars out of their hot-water bath. What's up?" As mayor of Stony Point, Ian's news could encompass too many possibilities to try to guess.

"I have two visitors sitting next to Charlotte's desk. They've come about the messages you left at the Highland Games. Can you come down and meet with us?"

Annie couldn't hold back a squeal. "Really?" A thought darted into her mind. "Wow, and in the fog too? It seems like a mighty strange day to decide to respond." Her eyes strayed over to the timer. "I'll leave as soon as I can take the jars out of the bath."

"Don't try to rush the driving," Ian told her. "I'll keep our guests entertained until you can get here."

"Thank you, Ian! Don't worry, I'll be careful. See you soon." Annie hung up the phone and dashed upstairs to prepare to leave as soon as the jars were set out to cool on a towel. The timer began to buzz while she was on her way back down the stairs, her hair combed, clothes changed, and teeth freshly brushed. Setting the bag containing the sealskin sporran containing the ferrules on the kitchen table, Annie swiftly transferred the jars of pickles out of the water and onto the counter. A moment later, after donning a light rain jacket against the moisture outside, she dashed out the door, fog or no fog.

Although it seemed to Annie she was inching laboriously along Ocean Drive toward town, she arrived at Town Hall within minutes. She hurried up the steps, through the main door and across the foyer, praying the visitors had not been hit with cold feet while waiting for her. She paused as she came to the mayor's office, taking a deep breath to calm herself before entering.

Ian's secretary, Charlotte Nash, sat behind a computer that dominated the right side of her desk. She looked up from the screen and smiled, as she swiveled her chair around to face the newcomer. Annie was surprised to see no other people in the room, and she fought disappointment.

"Hi, Annie," Charlotte's short silver hair bobbed as she nodded toward the door of the inner office. "The visitors are with the mayor. You can go right in."

Relief flooded Annie as she shed her outerwear and hung it on a coat tree in the corner by the door. With a quick "Thanks, Charlotte!" she strode to Ian's door and knuckled a light rap on it. At Ian's response, she stepped inside the office, closing the door behind her.

A man and a woman sat in front of Ian's desk, the man with dark hair and the woman with a layered, shoulder length cut, her light brown locks shining with gold highlights. There was something familiar about the man, although Annie was not yet in a position to see his face.

Ian's smile widened as he looked up at Annie. "Welcome, Annie. You made it in good time. How's the fog?"

"Still as thick and gray as Boots's fur," Annie answered. "But I'm starting to get used to it."

Ian addressed the newcomers. "Annie lived most of her adult life in Texas, but we're thankful to have her grace Stony Point now. Annie, this is Ansley Gunn Bell, and you might recognize Finley Rose."

Gunn, Bell and Rose! Annie maneuvered around the back of the chairs and approached the man and woman to offer her hand. Looking into Ansley's eyes, she almost felt as though she already knew her and realized why. "You must be related to Kyla Bell."

The woman, who appeared to be about ten years younger than Annie, smiled up at her. "Yes, Kyla is my daughter."

"She was a delight to meet and talk with," said Annie. "She gave such encouragement to the daughter of one of my friends."

"You must mean Emily." Ansley answered. "Kyla has talked about her since the Games. I think she would be thrilled to adopt her as a sister, especially since she doesn't have any."

A light laugh escaped Annie. "I have no doubt Emily feels the same way. She was so excited to meet her favorite dancer from the competition. Oh!" Annie caught her breath. "Did Kyla get her shoes back? Emily was beside herself with fear she wouldn't. We tried to find her to return them when she left them behind at the sheepherding field, but the crowds were too much so we left them at the lost and found booth."

"Yes, she did," Ansley reassured her. "And Kyla told me to pass on a message of thanks to all of you and to tell Emily she loved the note and the drawings. She wanted to come today, but I thought it better for her to stay home this time."

"I'll be sure to tell Emily," said Annie. "It will make her day." She moved closer to the man and held out her hand. "I'm pleased to meet you, Mr. Rose. My friends and I were very impressed with your falconry demonstration."

She was relieved when Finley reached out to accept her hand, his grip firm yet gentle. A shimmer of embarrassment tinted his dark cerulean eyes. "Thank you, Annie. You're being most kind, considering my actions on the day of the Highland Games. You and your friends caught me totally by surprise, and I didn't handle it well. Please forgive me."

Annie gave the man's hand a light squeeze before letting go. "Of course I forgive you, Finley. I am, however, extremely thankful that you have your eagle so well-trained. She is quite frightening when she swoops so close!"

"It was a foolish thing for me to do." The sincerity in the man's eyes was obvious. "Athena *is* exceptionally well-trained. She took to training immediately from the first day I began working with her. But she is still a wild animal for all that, and it was unwise for me to use her in the way I did."

Annie moved over to the free chair and sat. "May I ask why our questions prompted such a response, Finley? They seemed to cause shudders from one end of the Games to the other."

Ansley looked at her companion, as if asking permission. When the man nodded, she reached into her purse. "Fin and the others were not acting for themselves, but trying to protect two of their loved ones." She pulled her hand free, opening it up as she held it out for Annie and Ian to see. On her palm lay another ferrule bearing the hawk and rose. The set from Annie's attic was now complete. "I was one of them."

"And my mother was the second," Fin finished.

After a moment of silence, Ian asked, his voice gentle. "Did the bagpipe belong to you, Ansley?"

Ansley took a deep breath and answered, her voice tinged with sorrow. "No, it did not. It belonged to Fin's brother, Toren." She moved her gaze over to the man sitting beside her.

"Tor was my younger brother," Fin continued. "While my interest has always been falconry, Tor's was music—bagpipe music to be specific. He played so well you'd swear you were standing on a Munro mountain in the Highlands with the wind whipping around you. It felt like he played that way from the time he was still small."

Annie was reminded of a comment the pipe-maker MacTavish had made about a young piper. His voice had also held a shade of sadness. "Did Mr. MacTavish know Tor?"

"Yes, my mother had him build Tor's first set of pipes," Fin answered. "My mother created the design of the hawk and rose, and commissioned a silversmith to make the ferrules for it. My family has been involved in falconry for generations, and she was paying homage to it."

Before either Ian or Annie could respond to the new information, the pendulum clock on the wall of the office chimed the noon hour. The reminder of the time jerked Annie from her thoughts, and she looked apologetically at the visitors. "Oh no—I've lost track of time. I had made prior plans to meet a friend for lunch, and I completely forgot to warn her that I could be quite late." She turned to include Ian. "If you'll excuse me for just a moment, I need to give Alice a quick call." She rose to step outside the office. Both Ian and Finley stood as well.

Ian held up his hand indicating for her to wait. "I have an idea. Ansley and Fin, would you join us for lunch? The good folks at The Cup & Saucer would be glad to deliver for us, and we can use the conference room for our meal."

He saw Annie's eyebrow rise and answered the question in her eyes with his next sentences. "Annie's best friend, Alice MacFarlane, was with us at the Games and has been helping Annie solve the mystery of the sporran and ferrules found in her attic. If it is agreeable to you both, perhaps Annie could invite Alice to join us?"

The two visitors were quiet, their eyes meeting. Ansley inclined her head toward Ian. "I appreciate the hospitality, especially on such short notice, Mr. Butler. If Fin is agreeable to Alice joining us for lunch, I'm pleased to have her invited."

Annie attempted to look as casual as possible, as she didn't wish to put pressure on Fin's response. But although she was sure he had been sincere in his apology, she wasn't as sure he'd accept adding Alice to the visit.

With one more look into Ansley's brown eyes, Fin finally nodded. "Can I assume she was with you when Athena harried you?"

Relieved, Annie answered, "Yes, you assume correctly."

"Then I'd welcome her presence so that I may apologize to her personally," Fin said. He settled back in his chair.

"Thank you both," Annie said as she started again for the door, digging her cellphone out of her bag. She almost paused to suggest that her friend could stop by the diner to pick up lunch but thought better of it. Perhaps Peggy would be sent and yet another sleuthing friend would be alerted to the developments in the mystery. "I'll be just a moment." As she shut the door behind her, she saw Ian reach into his desk for a copy of the diner's menu.

Since Charlotte took her lunch promptly at noon, the outer office was empty. Annie walked back and forth as she waited for Alice to answer.

"Hey, Annie. You're not calling to cancel are you?" Alice's voice sounded in her ear.

"No, but I have a slight change in plans to suggest," answered Annie. "Instead of meeting me at the diner, come to Ian's office."

Annie could hear the puzzlement in her friend's voice. "Um, why? Have they added a salad bar in Town Hall—and finally gotten some decent coffee?"

"Because the falconer from the Highland Games is sitting in Ian's office as I speak, and he brought someone else with him. I think you'd like to hear the conversation over lunch, wouldn't you?" Annie grinned, imagining the look on her friend's face.

"Are you serious? What a crazy day to come! The man must have fog fever. Who's the other person?"

"Kyla Bell's mother. You'll see the resemblance as soon as you see her." Annie told her the plans for lunching in the conference room. "Charlotte is at lunch, of course, so just head to the room."

"OK." Annie could hear the sounds of her friend preparing to leave her house, the jangle of keys. "This is so exciting! I'll be there as soon as I can."

"I'll tell Ian. Do you trust us to order your lunch?" Annie thought to ask before she disconnected.

Her friend chuckled. "Just this once. And you'd better not mess it up."

"Considering how often we eat at The Cup & Saucer

together, I think you'll be safe." Annie said goodbye and closed her phone.

Pausing before the door to Ian's office, she closed her eyes and silently prayed that the truth would be a blessing to everyone involved.

17

When Annie re-entered the office, Ian looked up from the writing pad on the desk before him. "Is Alice coming? If so, what should we order for her?"

"Yes, she is," Annie answered. "She's on her way. For the order, somehow it feels like a day for soup. Order us both a cup of fish chowder and a side salad. Dressing on the side, of course."

Ian was no stranger to dining with Annie and Alice, and knew what dressings each lady preferred. He jotted down the information. "I'll call in the order."

"Don't forget to ask if Peggy can deliver it," Annie cautioned him. At times her friend's intense curiosity could rise to uncomfortable levels, but on this occasion Annie didn't want her to miss the chance to meet Ansley and Finley, even if she couldn't stay long.

Ian picked up the phone, mouthing "will do" to Annie. Returning to her chair, Annie sat again next to Ansley. "How long did it take for you to drive to Stony Point?" she asked the visitors.

"In today's fog, almost ninety minutes," Fin answered. "But it's usually a good twenty minutes less than that on normal days."

"I thought unpredictable was Maine's normal," Annie quipped. "But I must confess I find the capriciousness rather exciting most of the time. Of course, Texas has its wild side also, but it's drastically different from here. I'm enjoying those differences."

Ansley had not yet put the ferrule away, but instead she toyed with it, turning it over and running a finger over the engraving. "I've never lived anywhere but Maine. I still live in the same county where I was born, even." A soft smile touched her mouth. "Guess I'm just a homebody."

Ian set the phone back in the handset. "The food should be here in about fifteen minutes … with Peggy."

Annie clasped her hands together. "Oh, good! Peggy is Emily's mother, and she will be so happy to meet you, Ansley. Were you working at one of the venues at the Games?"

"No, I wasn't able to attend," Ansley answered. "My husband's mother has been ill and had to be hospitalized the night before the Games. She begged me to stay with her. I couldn't say no, though I hated to miss Kyla's dancing."

"Oh, I'm sorry to hear that." Annie briefly placed a hand over Ansley's fidgeting one. "How is she doing now?"

"Better, thank you," Ansley said. "She's gained some strength and has been home for a week. It was touch-and-go for a while." She paused for a moment. "I had hoped to respond to your note sooner, but this was the first day I felt comfortable leaving her for the day."

"Ans was determined too," Fin inserted. "She was not going to let a bit of fog keep her from coming." He quirked a smile in her direction. "I wouldn't have let her come alone today, even if I hadn't already planned to accompany her on whichever day she was able to come to Stony Point."

"Well, we're very glad you did," said Ian. "Driving a

distance in fog like this is dangerous enough when you're alone. Hopefully, the fog will lift by the time you head back home."

Annie glanced at the clock on the wall. "Alice should be here soon. Perhaps we should move over to the conference room."

"Yes, let's get settled there before the food comes." Ian stood and escorted his guests out of his office and down the hall to the large room outfitted with a long table surrounded by generously cushioned seats. The mayor had always maintained that town board members could work harder and longer only if they were physically comfortable.

The guests selected chairs across from each other; Annie sat next to Ansley and Ian beside Fin. They had all adjusted their seats and were sitting back when the door opened.

"Hi!" Alice shut the door behind her and approached the table. Settling her smiling blue eyes on the visitors, she said to them, "Thank you for allowing me to crash the party."

"Alice, this is Ansley Bell," Ian began the introductions. "Ansley, this is Alice MacFarlane, another lifelong resident of Maine like yourself."

Ansley extended her hand to the newcomer. "I'm so happy to meet you, Alice. I apologize for interrupting your lunch plans."

"Oh, please don't worry," Alice told her. "I'm thrilled you were able to come, whenever you could."

Annie briefly informed her friend of the reason for Ansley's delay in responding to her message.

"What a blessing for you to be near your mother-in-law

during her illness." Empathy shone in Alice's eyes.

Ian gestured to his right, where the other visitor was seated. "And you will remember Finley Rose, Alice."

Having been prepared by her phone conversation with Annie, no surprise showed on Alice's face. She held out her hand to the falconer. "Welcome to Stony Point." She exaggerated peering around the room. "Did you bring Athena with you?"

A wry, but thankful, grin spread across Fin's face. "Fear not, she's at home today." His face grew more serious, and he asked Alice's forgiveness for the event outside the food tent at the Highland Games, as he had with Annie and Ian.

"It may surprise you, Fin, but I've been known to exhibit impetuous behavior every once in a while," Alice said, her eyes daring Annie and Ian to laugh. "I certainly forgive you, although I hope we are to learn the full reason behind your decision to use Athena on that Saturday."

Ansley answered for him. "You will, as soon as lunch arrives so there are no interruptions."

"It's a rather long story," Fin added.

"Just the kind I prefer on a foggy day." Alice rubbed her hands together in anticipation before turning away to take a seat.

Once she was seated, Ian looked at his long-time friend. "Alice, I ordered you a large coffee with lunch. I hope you don't mind."

She cocked her head at him. "Now Mayor, what I would have minded is if you had forced me to drink the Town Hall coffee. That would simply be cruel and unusual punishment." Aside to Ansley and Fin, Alice added, "Poor Ian, he's consumed so much of the bad stuff, his taste buds must be permanently crippled."

"If you have any suggestions for a new coffee vendor, Alice, please feel free to pass on the information to Charlotte," said Ian. "Just keep in mind the town does run on a budget, and our constituents may not appreciate additional taxes for caffeine fixes."

"I'll see what I can find and let Charlotte know. Seeing as she's a tea woman, it makes sense she wouldn't know bad coffee from good." Over the years, Alice had learned how to enjoy the finer things in life on a tight budget. She relished the idea of passing on her hard-won knowledge to the mayor's secretary.

Three staccato raps thumped at the door, and Ian rose to open it. "Hi, Peggy. Thanks for delivering for us," he said, spreading the door wide to make room for the waitress and the large box she carried. She hadn't bothered to cover her pink uniform or her hair for the dash across the street in the fog, and her dark hair glistened faintly like she was wearing a fog hairnet. "Can I take that from you?"

"Nah, Mr. Mayor," Peggy would have waved him off, had her arms been free. She bustled over to the table and set the box at one end. Once relieved of the bulk, her eyes moved around the table as she shared a smile with everyone. When they reached Fin, however, her eyes widened in surprise. "Why, you look familiar!" the words popped out unbidden.

"Finley, this is Peggy Carson, Emily's mother," said Annie, trying to give her friend time to recover. "Peggy, this is Finley Rose. Fin and Ansley Bell, who is Kyla's mother, have come because of my messages."

The waitress's hands hovered over the box, pausing in their readiness to pull out the food as her smile widened to a grin. "Thanks for coming! I had almost given up hope!" She turned to Ian, "Is that why the boss insisted I make the delivery instead of Breck? Clever, Mr. Mayor, very clever."

She reached into the box and pulled out several round cups with secure tops, setting them on the table. "These are the fish chowders. Who wanted them?" Annie, Alice, and Ansley motioned to claim the aromatic soup. Next came a wrapped sandwich. "Tuna salad—which must be yours, Mr. Mayor." She handed the sandwich to Ian and dove back into the box. "So the club special must be … Finley's."

As the man reached out to take the wrapped meal, he said to Peggy, "Please, call me Fin. Pretty much everyone does, unless I'm giving a demonstration. And please forgive me for my shenanigans with Athena. It was a dimwitted thing to do."

"I appreciate your apology, Fin," Peggy responded plainly, "and of course I forgive you." She passed out side salads to the three who had ordered the chowder, along with packets of saltines. "Now for the drinks." She paused for effect and then started removing coffee cups from the box. "Four coffees. Sorry, Alice, only one for you this time, but it is large." Last came a cold beverage cup. "And one Coke."

"The Coke is mine," Fin said.

The waitress wagged a finger at him. "You may regret it when you see what's for dessert."

"I'll take my chances." Fin gave her a bad-boy smile.

Ansley laughed and said, "Fin's one of those disgusting people who can eat anything he wants, and he never gains an ounce. Even with a sweet tooth."

Peggy let out a loud sigh. "Fin, I can forgive you for sending your eagle to scare us, but I'm not sure I can forgive *that*!" She turned back to Ian. "There are plenty of plates and forks in the box for when you're ready for them. I guess I should get back to the diner, it being lunch rush and all." She peered at each of her Stony Point friends. "If someone doesn't call me after work and tell me more, I'll come banging on your doors—see if I don't. It's going to be hard enough concentrating as it is!"

"We wouldn't think of it," Annie reassured her friend. "We wish you could stay but wanted you at least to see for yourself what resulted from our day at the Highland Games."

Peggy nodded and turned to the visitors and said, "Don't you two be strangers around here. Emily would be overjoyed to have a visit with Kyla and see her dance again."

"Kyla would love that too," said Ansley. "If you can wait another minute, I'll write down our contact information." She reached into her purse and drew out a small pad with a pen.

Peggy's face brightened. "Sure." She waved a hand at the others. "Dig in, everybody. The food's not getting any warmer, you know."

"Yes, sir!" Alice saluted her friend and popped the lid off her chowder, stirring it with a plastic soup spoon. She leaned forward for a spill-free taste and then declared, "Delicious, as usual."

Ansley tore off the sheet of paper, folded it in half, and

handed it to Peggy. "We'd love to have Emily come visit us on the farm. My husband, Kyle, built her a platform in one of the barns for dancing. Your daughter might like to see it."

Peggy slipped the paper into one of the pockets of her apron. "Just be warned: We might not be able to drag Em away from your barn. She'd dance all day and night if she didn't have school and need sleep." "Thanks for braving the fog to come," she said, glancing at Fin and including him in her farewell. "Enjoy the food!" Peggy left the room much less burdened than when she had arrived, in more ways than one, and she sang under her breath as she hurried back to The Cup & Saucer.

After the door closed, Ansley removed the lid from her salad bowl. "When my brother, Leathan, came home after the Games and told me about your questions regarding his cantle's design, and then Fin showed up with the note you had written him, my first response was to let it go—to ignore it. Then after they had both left, Kyla danced in, full of chatter about this little dancer she had met and how nice the whole group from Stony Point was. She had more words for all of you than for her first-place award in dance! Taking first in the Premier group as a twelve-year-old is very unusual, so you should take her exuberance as a compliment. It made me think twice about doing nothing." She tipped the small container of vinaigrette over the bowl and drizzled it on the greens.

Fin swallowed a bite of his club sandwich. "Ans really surprised me when she told me she wanted to come and share everything. Now that I've met you, I can see she made the right choice."

"Fin, you mentioned your mother as the second reason you reacted the way you did at the Games. Why?" asked Ian carefully. "If you'd rather wait until after you've finished eating, we understand."

Fin shook his head. "No need. You may have noticed when we first mentioned my brother, we said he used to play the bagpipes." Ian, Annie, and Alice solemnly nodded. "Tor died in January of 1986, while he was participating in extreme sports in Colorado. Our mother has never recovered from it."

"I'm so sorry to hear that." Annie's voice was soft. "I can't imagine losing my daughter."

Fin bowed his head briefly, acknowledging her sympathy. "My father kept thinking her grief would lessen in time, so he kept the bagpipes and other personal items in Tor's room at home and simply shut the door."

"Do you know how the ferrules and sporran ended up in Annie's attic?" asked Alice. She spooned some chowder to her lips.

Fin nodded, setting his cup on the table. "I never knew exactly what had happened to them and had to do some quiet detective work myself, making sure my mother didn't hear about it. We have to go back to 1978 to give you the foundation."

"That's the year the Highland Games started, isn't it?" asked Ian.

"Yes," answered Fin. "My family has always been very close to the Gunn family. Our farms are adjacent to each other, and we always had picnics and played sports together, like one giant family."

Ansley spoke up, her fork poised in midair. "So of course our families not only entered as many of the Highland Games competitions as possible, but also made up their own spin on it. My dad donated his sealskin sporran as a trophy of sorts, to the family who collectively brought home the most honors at the Games. The triumphant family would display the sporran prominently until the next Games. It was a crazy, fun time for us each year."

"The competition grew to other Scot families in the area, as well," added Fin. "In the last year, I think we had seven or eight families vying for the prize. We were all so evenly matched, the sporran changed hands often."

"Do you know which family had it the final year?" asked Ian.

"Yes, we Roses won it that year," answered Fin. "But we don't have it now. The August after Tor died, my mother was still so distraught, my father returned the sporran to Mr. Gunn." He glanced over at Ansley.

Annie had quietly been following the story, melding it with her grandpa's journal entry. She added, "And Mr. Gunn then gave it to my grandfather, Charles Holden, his veterinarian."

Both Ansley and Fin were startled. "How did you know?" Fin blurted.

Annie gave them a sheepish look. "After I came home from the Games, I doubted I'd ever hear from anyone. So I did the last thing I could think of, which was to read through my grandfather's vet journals. He kept notes on his practice every year until his retirement. In the 1986 book there was an entry about tending a sheep with an abscess at the Gunn farm." She paused, a glance darting toward Alice. "He mentioned the sporran."

Ansley stared at her coffee cup, nodding slowly. "I can see my dad doing that. He trusted your grandfather completely—trust built through years of bonding over the animals. He attended Dr. Holden's funeral." She shook her head at the realization.

"Grandpa always said you can tell a lot about a person by how they treat animals," Annie said. "What I still don't know from his journal is why the ferrules were in the sporran." She looked at the visitors. "Do you know?"

Fin brushed sandwich crumbs from his fingers. "My father told me he had the silver hawk-and-rose ferrules removed from Tor's bagpipe, reassembled it with regular ferrules, and gave the bagpipe to another family friend for safekeeping. He put the ferrules in the sporran."

"And the family friend was ... ?" Alice asked, raising an eyebrow.

Ansley answered, "Logan Bell."

The three Stony Point friends were silent for a moment, knowing the next logical question most likely would tread on very personal ground for Ansley. Ian gave the slightest of nods to Annie, feeling it should be her who asked it.

Annie reached over and placed a hand upon one of Ansley's. "Then why do you have a solitary ferrule with the design?"

The woman's eyes grew distant, yet soft, as she returned to the very young woman she once was. She whispered, "I took one ferrule from the sporran. I heard Dad talking to Dr. Holden on the phone, saying he had a special request to make of him. Something told me it had to do with the sporran, and I had to keep something ... " Her voice caught, and she paused before continuing, "... something to remember Tor by. He was, after all, my first love."

18

The room remained quiet in reverence to the memories their visitors were sharing.

"You should have seen Tor when he was playing his music," said Fin. "He had all the girls swooning … but he could never take his eyes off of Ans."

Ansley spread her hands out in front of her on the table, pushing the empty containers away. "Tor and I grew up together. Fin was a bit older and busy with kids his own age, so Tor and I hung out all the time." The wisp of a smile floated across her face and lips. "He played, and I danced—for hours on end. He could be the most charming boy. When we got older, I fell in love with him. All the girls around envied me, but they didn't see all of Tor."

"Tor had a wild streak," Fin told the group solemnly. "He was funny and kind, but he also loved the thrill of challenging limits. If there was a locked gate, he would climb it. A speed limit? He would break it. A cliff? He would dive off it. I tried to keep an eye on him, at first. But then I went away to college and couldn't be there. By the time I graduated, I knew there was no way I could rein him in anymore." He frowned down at the table, his hands clinched.

"We dated for two years," Ansley continued. "At first I was convinced Tor was my soul mate, and we were bonded by the love of music and each other. But in the second year, his recklessness just exploded, and he became erratic. It got to where I never knew what to expect when he picked me up for a date. He didn't play his pipes as much, and at the end, he only played it for family events and the Highland Games." Her voice dropped to a whisper once again. "After the '85 Games, I told him I couldn't take living in fear for him anymore and broke off the relationship." She shook her head. "Of course, I didn't stop worrying about him, and I still loved him. I thought maybe it would wake him up and help him see how he needed to change things."

"The problem was, Tor didn't want to change," Fin picked up the story. "He threw off what little restraint he had when he was with Ansley and went looking for barriers he could break. Finally, he embraced extreme sports. Instead of diving off cliffs into the ocean, he was diving out of airplanes with skis on and plummeting down mountainsides." He breathed in a long, slow breath—and then released it. "Deep down, I don't think anyone was surprised when the call came about Tor's accident. And I think it's partly why my mother has had such a hard time recovering from it. She saw it was coming, but she was powerless to do anything about it."

After sitting motionless for a couple of minutes as the weightiness of past events washed over them all, Annie reached for her bag. Taking the sporran from it, she handed it to Ansley. "My grandfather wrote in the his journal, 'The sealskin goes to the one who bears the falcon and the rose.' Following his direction, I'm happy for you to have it."

The woman ran her hand along the sleek fur. "Thank

you. Perhaps my family is ready to have it back in our care. I can't thank your grandfather, but I can sincerely thank all of you for your help and care ..." she said, managing a weak smile toward Fin, "no matter how some of us treated you."

Fin reached across the table to grasp her hand, squeezing it gently. "You Gunns have always been a good balance to us—uh—more dramatic Roses."

Alice's head jerked up at his comment. "That's right! You must be related to McKenna Rose."

"Guilty as charged," Finn confessed, "although I had little say in the matter. She's my sister."

"She certainly did inherit a flair for the dramatic," Ian said diplomatically.

Alice leaned forward, looked Fin in the eyes. "I've been trying to figure out if McKenna was trying to spur us on in our search or scare the tarnation out of us. Do you know?"

"McKenna was being her typical enigmatic self," he answered. "She told me she thought the truth needed to come out. After all, you had definitely found the sporran and ferrules, and there was nothing we could do about that, short of theft."

Annie's friends turned to look at her. "Been there, done that," muttered Alice. "Thank you for not trying it. It's beginning to be a bit cliché."

Ansley gasped. "Have you been robbed before, Annie?"

"There have been attempts," Annie admitted. "Let's just say I'm thankful we have a dedicated police force here." She grinned. "I'm also thankful I didn't have to call on them this time. They could use a vacation like the rest of us."

Alice's gaze moved over to Ian and back to Fin. "Did

McKenna happen to mention flirting as one of her tactics to get our attention?"

While a light flush crept across the mayor's face, Fin casually shrugged. "Noooo, she didn't, but it sounds like her. She's not above playing a part or using her charms, if she thinks it will enhance the value of her performance. Or in this case, grab the attention of people she wants to make sure are listening."

Alice guffawed. "Well, I must admit that it was effective for that. But why didn't she let us talk to her, after working so hard to get our attention? Did she tell you how she ran out on us?"

Fin nodded. "She did. She felt the story wasn't hers to tell, so she was just trying to keep your curiosity peaked so you would keep looking and asking."

"Too bad McKenna didn't know Annie," Ian said, recovering enough to laugh. "It would have saved her all the dramatic efforts. Annie never stops looking until her mysteries are solved."

Annie raised her right hand. "What can I say? Blame it on all those Trixie Belden and Nancy Drew books I read as a kid. I hope McKenna will be pleased to hear the truth has, indeed, come out, and that the sporran has been returned to its rightful place."

Ansley opened the cantle of the sporran, reaching inside to remove the ferrules. She stretched her hand, ferrules nestled in the palm, across the table toward Fin. "These belong to your family, Fin." Pausing for a moment, a mental battle plain on her face, she then added the ferrule she had kept with her all those years. "All of them. Maybe someday you'll be able to put them back on Tor's pipes and pass them on to the younger generation of Clan Rose."

Fin's dark eyes stared into hers, decades of sorrow and guilt etched in their depths, yet leaving room for something else now: hope. He picked up one of the ferrules in his long fingers and placed it back in Ansley's hand. "Mother is still in our home, and I don't know that she'll ever be ready to hear Tor's pipes play."

The slow dawning of an idea cast light onto the contours of Fin's thin face. He added the rest of the ferrules to the single one in Ansley's hand. "Dad entrusted the pipes to your father-in-law. Perhaps it's time to return the ferrules to their original place, to be ready for the day when the pipes will be freely played again. Will you make sure they are restored?"

"I will," Ansley answered, her voice quiet, yet strong. As she closed her fingers over the bands, Annie and Alice both dipped their heads to swipe at the moisture threatening to spill over from their eyes.

The jumble of miscellany Annie had inherited from her grandparents had brought much adventure of kinds she could never have imagined when she first arrived from Texas. She had to admit sometimes the finds brought danger. But other times, like this day, they brought healing or at least began the healing process. The three from Stony Point deeply felt the privilege of sharing the moment.

"I don't know about the rest of you," Ian said, after an appropriate amount of time, "but I think this occasion calls for fresh raspberry pie, straight from Marie's oven."

"Excellent idea," Fin agreed. Ansley smiled her

concurrence. Alice joined Ian at the end of the table to help serve the pie Peggy had brought from The Cup & Saucer.

When a slice sat before each person, Ian nipped a piece onto his fork and raised it like a glass of champagne. "Here's to sweeter times ahead!"

"Here, here!" the others chimed before slipping the treat into their mouths. For a time, silence again overtook the group as they enjoyed the treat. Then Annie broached a subject she had been considering since hearing the whole story of the Gunns and Roses. "I have one more question for you, Ansley and Fin."

Alice quipped, "Only one? Are you sure?"

"Only one." Annie nodded decisively.

Fin was gathering the last delicious crumbs of his pie with his plastic fork. "Lay it on us, Annie."

"I've been thinking ... ," Annie began. Her eyes dared her friends to add commentary. "It's obvious to me from the way your families acted when I came around with my photos and the ferrule at the Games that you are all still very much connected and close." She paused. "Ansley, your father canceled the seven-year tradition in order to help Fin's mother in her grieving process, right?"

Ansley nodded. "But I'm sure Dad had no idea how long Mrs. Rose's process was going to last."

"It has stunned all of us," added Fin.

Annie continued. "Would you and your families consider restoring the annual sporran competition in the spirit of healing, remembrance, and friendship? I realize that for some people, like Mrs. Rose, remembrance is torture, but it can also bring joy from sorrow as we celebrate the unique gift of every life, whether a long or short one."

Annie told them about the days she had spent rocking on her porch in Texas after her husband, Wayne, died. Doubts and despondency had nagged at her, and it had not been until she allowed herself the freedom to embrace life again—taking an unexpected path to a little seaside village in Maine—that she had been able to truly honor her husband's memory rather than wearing it like a suicide vest around her heart. Ansley and Fin listened intently, nodding in recognition.

When Annie concluded her story, Ansley and Fin sat quiet for a while as the three friends relaxed against the backs of their comfortable chairs, marveling at how everything at the Highland Games had come together to bring them all to this moment in the Stony Point Town Hall. No matter what the Gunn, Rose, and Bell families decided, the friends were thankful.

Fin was the first to speak. "Your idea of restoring the competition has never entered my mind, to be honest." He glanced over at his longtime friend. "Ans, I think we should seriously consider it, and then discuss it with the rest of the families." He returned his gaze to Annie. "What you told us about your grief for your husband hits home, Annie. Sadly, I don't know if anyone has ever approached my mother in that way about Tor's death. It might not help, but maybe it would. Thank you for sharing it."

"Yes—thank you, Annie," said Ansley. "You've given us lots to think about today. I appreciate it more than I can express." She cradled the ferrules in her hand. "I'll start by taking these and the pipes to Mr. MacTavish to have them refitted."

Alice smiled. "Very fitting—no pun intended."

Fin glanced at his watch. "Ans, we should get going. Afternoon chores are waiting. Thank you for lunch, Ian, and opening up your office to us on the spur of the moment. If there's anything I can ever do for you, please let me know."

"That goes for me too," Ansley added.

"Now that you mention it," Ian began with a grin, "just last night the town board voted to plan a Robert Burns Dinner for next January. We could use some fine Highland dancing for the event." Annie and Alice perked up their heads.

"Wonderful! I'm so glad it went through," exclaimed Annie.

"It's going to be so much fun!" Alice added on the heels of Annie's reaction.

Ansley turned her smile to each of her new friends. "I know Kyla will be overjoyed to perform for the dinner. Let me check to make sure her dance teacher hasn't already scheduled her troupe before confirming with you."

"Excellent," said Ian. He reached over to shake Fin's hand. "I hope we'll see you again soon in our fair town."

"Maybe even with Athena," Alice added, with a mischievous wink, "as long as you don't set her off on anyone."

"Deal." Fin laughed and stood up.

The trio escorted Ansley and Fin to the front door of the Town Hall, relieved to see the fog had thinned out some in the early afternoon. As the two visitors disappeared down the front steps, Ian turned to Annie and Alice. "Now, that's what I call a good day at work."

"Amen!" exclaimed Annie. "You know, Ian, since the town board approved the Robert Burns Dinner, I'm going to need your measurements soon. Brianna Kincaid is coming to A Stitch in Time in a few weeks, and now we can ask her to help us make the kilts for January."

Alice informed Ian, "Brianna told us the measurements need to be taken by someone other than the person being measured. So you'd better let Annie take them."

Annie suddenly needed to examine the contents of her bag, keeping her eyes away from both her impish best friend and Ian.

"Since I have no wish to show up at the dinner wearing a lopsided kilt, I will bow to Brianna's expert advice," Ian responded casually. He addressed Annie. "Why don't you stop by the morning of the meeting? I'm always at work before nine."

Annie drew her gaze out from her bag and let it brush by Ian's ruggedly handsome face. "Sure. I'll text you when I'm on my way as a reminder." She dug into her bag again, this time in earnest, pulling out her car keys. "Thank you for being our contact for Fin and Ansley—and for lunch."

"It was my pleasure," Ian said. "You two drive safely." He opened the outer door for them.

"See you soon, Ian." Alice called as she followed Annie outside. Before she turned to the right to head for her car, she asked her friend, "May I ride with you on the morning of Brianna's demonstration?"

Annie nodded, somewhat surprised as she usually did just that. "Of course. Why the need to ask now?"

"Just wanted to make sure," Alice answered. "You have such a pretty blush going now; I didn't want to miss the opportunity to see it again."

"Maybe I'll just let you take the mayor's measurements," Annie called after her friend, giving her a look similar to the one she turned on Boots after discovering the cat's hijinks. "And don't forget: measure twice; cut once." Chuckling, she looked both ways and dashed across the street toward her Malibu, waving goodbye to her friend behind her.

* * * *

In early October, Annie once again dashed across the street from Town Hall toward A Stitch in Time, Ian's measurements written in her notebook. This time Alice was beside her, having thoroughly enjoyed watching the interplay between her best friend and the mayor. Alice had behaved, if she did say so herself. Over the weeks, she had come to the realization she had become too heavy-handed in teasing her two friends and decided to stop. She was confident Annie and Ian would finally see what everyone else could and do something about it—when they were ready. Until then, there were plenty of other outlets for her sense of humor.

Pulling the door of the shop open, Annie paused as she saw the amount of people milling between the displays. "Wow!" she said to Alice over her shoulder. "Look at all of these women!"

"I could see and marvel better if you'd let me through the door," said Alice, laughing. After stepping over the threshold into the busy room as Annie moved forward, she added, "Mary Beth's advertising about the workshop sure paid off! I hope there's room for everyone."

Mary Beth hurried over to the two women. "Hey—could you two help Kate set up another table in the back? A circle of chairs up front won't do for this kind of class." As soon as her friends agreed, she thanked them and rushed to handle another task.

Annie and Alice wove between the gathering women, sharing waves and "hellos" to those they knew on their way to the back. Kate was wrestling with a long table, much too bulky for one person.

"Wait!" Alice admonished the younger woman. "You're a back injury just waiting to happen." She and Annie rushed to help Kate extend the legs and set it upright, creating a U shape with the two tables already in place.

Kate brushed her hands on her shop apron. "Thanks, you two! We were caught a little by surprise, if you couldn't tell."

"We were amazed when we came through the door," said Annie. "It's obvious Ian's idea of having a Robert Burns Dinner struck a chord with the townsfolk."

Kate exclaimed, "I'll say! Getting Brianna to come was a stroke of genius." Her easy smile reflected her thanks to her friends for their part.

"Ah, there are my former students!" Brianna's voice made the three women turn around.

They hurried over. "Welcome, Brianna!" Alice's voice rang out. "I hope you're ready for our rowdy Stony Point bunch."

Brianna turned around to show them what hung from her shoulder, a large bag stuffed to bulging. "I come prepared for anything! And there's more in the van." She turned back to Annie and Alice. "May I borrow you two for some help with unloading? I planned to arrive earlier, but was delayed by an accident outside of Bath."

The two friends hurried with Brianna to where her van was parked. Before loading their arms with items for the class, she reached over and grabbed something from the dashboard. She handed it to Annie. "A friend of mine asked me to deliver this to you both."

Curiosity on her face, Annie turned the envelop over first to note how it was addressed. Written in lovely, flowing calligraphy were the names of those from Stony Point who had attended the Highland Games: Annie, Ian, Alice, Peggy, Wally, and Emily. Looking over her shoulder, Alice murmured. "How beautiful!" Annie quickly turned the envelope back over and slid a finger under the flap to open it.

She pulled out a thick square of paper adorned with a hand-painted falcon and rose. Underneath that, it bore the words:

"Your presence is hereby requested for the Bestowin' of the Sporran next year, directly following the Highland Games."